BROADWAY PLAY PUBLISHING, INC.

TARANTARA! TARANTARA!

by

Ian Taylor

Date Due

249 WE   563-3820

First presented by the Bristol Old Vic Company on May 20th, 1975. Subsequently presented at the Westminster Theatre, London, and the Phoenix Theatre, London, with the following cast of characters:

JOE, a stage hand .... Jonathan Darvill
RICHARD D'OYLY CARTE .... George Raistrick
JESSIE BOND .... Judith Coke
GERALDINE ULMAR .... Hazel McBride
ROSE HERVEY .... Sue Withers
SIR ARTHUR SULLIVAN .... Timothy Kightley
GEORGE GROSSMITH .... Mark Buffery
W.S. GILBERT .... Christopher Scoular
STAGE HANDS .... Roger Farrent, Julia Chambers,
                                   David Finlayson

The Play directed by David Horlock
Setting by John McMurray
Lighting by David Cohen

The play opens Back-stage at the Savoy Theatre on October 3rd, 1888

CASTING

This piece is meant to be performed in the spirit of pantomime, in fact it would suit this kind of entertainment very
well. Also, so long as the text is not interfered with, more
actors, or a bigger chorus could be used. Therefore, in the
case of a large company some people could be there just to
sing. The whole thing should be irreverent and at times
farcical.

SETTING

Permanently on stage are the following: GILBERT'S desk, with
chair or stool, and an umbrella stand; on the opposite side,
SULLIVAN'S podium, with music-stand and padded seat, and
a hat-stand, table and chair nearby; up C, CARTE'S table and
chair. A piano and stool are set where convenient, or may be
placed in the orchestra pit. One or two other bentwood chairs
as desired. Everything should be kept simple for fluid, swift
movement.

Furnishings and props for the excerpts from the various
operas may be as simple or as elaborate as facilities allow, and
are brought on or struck by the three stage hands, at the
appropriate moments.

MUSICAL NUMBERS

The "characters" in the operatic excerpts are played and sung
by members of the cast: the allocations are indicated at the
appropriate points in the text. The same procedure is followed
when the cast play other characters (*e.g.*, Geraldine Ulmar as
Helen Lenoir, see p. 24).

FURNITURE AND PROPERTIES

All that is strictly necessary for the operatic excerpts is a
suggestion (more or less elaborate as desired) of the characters
represented—*e.g.*, a wig for the JUDGE in *Trial by Jury* (see p.
19), a hat and jacket for CARTE and GILBERT to exchange in
H.M.S. Pinafore (see p. 40), etc.

ACT ONE

A MUSIC REHEARSAL FOR *THE YEOMEN OF THE GUARD*

The Pianist is playing, and JOE, *a Stage Hand, is sweeping the floor of the stage and whistling the music.* CARTE *enters and goes up to him.*

JOE: *(Cheerfully.)* Hello, Mr. Carte.

CARTE: Hello, Joe. Got this tune, then?

JOE: Yes, Mr. Carte. I know 'em all. I'm everyone's understudy.

CARTE: Everybody in rehearsal today?

*The actresses enter—*JESSIE BOND, GERALDINE ULMAR, *and* ROSE HERVEY. *They say "Hello" to* CARTE, *who sits on the edge of his desk. They take off their outdoor clothes and hand them to the Stage Hands, who take them off stage.*

JESSIE BOND *goes across to the Pianist.*

JESSIE: Mr. White, can you hear my first song before Sir Arthur arrives?

The Pianist plays the intro. CARTE *sits at his desk and works.* JESSIE *sings a few lines of "When a Maiden Loves" and then fluffs. She stops and swears under her breath.*

When maiden loves, she sits and sighs,
    She wanders to and fro
Unbidden tear-drops fill her eyes,
And to all her questions she replies
    With a sad "heigh-ho!"

Oh Gawd, I've gone and forgotten the words and I knew them this morning. Can I try it again, Mr. White? I've got to get this thing right. The curtains open and there's me sitting there at the spinning wheel. *(A broad hint at* CARTE). I can't think why they didn't use a chorus to open the show as they always do?

The Pianist plays again. JESSIE *reads her script.* SULLIVAN *enters, with rolls of music under his arm. The Pianist stops playing.*

SULLIVAN: Good afternoon, ladies and gentlemen.

ALL: Good afternoon, Sir Arthur.

SULLIVAN: Hello, Carte.

CARTE *nods and smiles, then continues working.* JOE *helps* SULLIVAN *take off his coat, which he hangs on the stand.*

SULLIVAN: *(As he is helped off with his coat.)* I am frightfully sorry if I've delayed everybody. I know we must make the most of these music rehearsals. *(A broad hint at* CARTE). They are so few and time's precious. Thank you, Mr. White. Is George Grossmith here?

JOE: George! You're wanted!

GROSSMITH *enters very nervously.* GROSSMITH *at this time needed drugs to keep going. He holds up a music sheet, shaking his head.*

GROSSMITH: I'll never get this one. *(He stops on seeing* CARTE.*)*

SULLIVAN: *(Giving him another sheet of music.)* We'll have a go at that one later. The one I'm worried about is your buffoon song. That is going to give us all a lot of trouble. I'd like to go through it with you before Mr. Gilbert arrives.

ALL: Ugh!

GROSSMAN: Oh. He is not coming in today?

ROSE: He's brought things grinding to a halt twice this week.

GERALDINE: Can't you keep him out, Mr. Carte?

JESSIE: Well, I'm ready for him this time, if he starts anything.

SULLIVAN: *(Almost sarcastically.)* There are one or two songs he's worried about.

GROSSMITH: That makes two of us.

SULLIVAN: Three of us. I still haven't been able to set the one with the Heighdy Chorus.

GROSSMITH: "I have a song to sing O." That one?

SULLIVAN: Yes. I have a song to set o—and I don't know how I'm going to do it.

CARTE *laughs—and waves as if to say "You'll do it, Arthur".*

SULLIVAN: No, really, it doesn't make any musical sense. *(He looks about to indulge in complaints about GILBERT's words then stops.)*

GROSSMITH: *(Very worriedly.)* But I will have it in time to learn it? I mean, I won't have the song just as I'm about to step on the stage like last time . . . ?

SULLIVAN: *(With charm.)* Yes, yes, George, you shall have it in plenty of time. You shall have the song even if I have to get Mr. Gilbert to set it himself.

CARTE *laughs.* SULLIVAN *laughs with him.*

GERALDINE: Heaven forbid. Sir Arthur.

SULLIVAN: Yes, Miss Ulmar.

GERALDINE: Will you hear the song I sing with Fairfax?

JESSIE: And mine.

ROSE: And mine.

SULLIVAN: Yes. Yes. I must hear all the songs I've set so far whilst I have the chance. But I'll hear George first. So when you are ready, George.

After some preparations, GROSSMITH *sings the first verse—"Oh a private buffoon is a light-hearted loon" (Refer to the music score for verse.)*

SULLIVAN: Yes, well, it'll be there, George, it'll be there. But I do prefer my tune! Let's try the last verse, shall we?

GROSSMITH *sings the last verse—"Though your head it may rack" (For words, refer to the music score, fifth verse.) During the singing of this verse* GILBERT *enters hobbling. He is very bad tempered.*

GROSSMITH: *(Singing.)* . . . "They don't blame you so long as you're funny."

GILBERT: *(Giving a roar of sarcastic laughter.)* Funny? Funny eh, Grossmith? Funny? It would be funny if we could hear the words. The words are funny. Bloody funny. If they're not garbled. And you are garbling, Grossmith. Garbling. I suppose this play will be like all the others before it, we'll hear *Sir* Arthur's music all right. Everybody will go into raptures over Sir Arthur's music, but of my words not a whit will be heard. Not a bloody whit. Now you've made me swear, Grossmith, and I don't like swearing when ladies are present.

JESSIE: Oh, don't mind us. Mr. Gilbert.

ACTRESSES: No, don't mind us . . .

JOE *helps* GILBERT *off with his coat.*

GILBERT: I'm not minding you. There are cleaning ladies in the building . . .

JESSIE: Oh, dear . . .

In turning away from JOE, GILBERT *bumps into the* ACTRESSES.

GILBERT: Kindly get out of the way and let me get to my desk. You're holding up my work . . .

JOE *hangs up* GILBERT'S *coat.*

JESSIE: Don't you speak to me like that!

ROSE: We're not chorus girls, you know!

GILBERT: Oh! Aren't you? Who took you out of the back row of the chorus? And I can put you back whenever I like.

JESSIE: *(Aside.)* Oh my Gawd. I'm going to ask for more money.

GILBERT: *(Overhearing the remark.)* You'll not get it. We'll have no stars here, Jessie Bond . . .

GILBERT *shuffles across to his desk. He glares at* CARTE *as acknowledgement and settles at his desk.* JESSIE *protests.*

SULLIVAN: *(Who has been studiously ignoring* GILBERT; *to* GROSSMITH) Thank you, George. Oh, Jessie, Jessie, if you come over here, please, I'll go through that opening song with you line by line until we get the rhythm of it.

GILBERT: *(From behind his desk.)* Wait a minute! Let me get up to the back there! If Jessie Bond is going to warble I want to be able to hear right up there, every word. Every syllable.

SULLIVAN: *(Suddenly breaking.)* Mr. Gilbert! This is a music rehearsal.

GILBERT: I am aware of that, sir!

SULLIVAN: And I am in charge of it.

GILBERT: You, sir, are in charge of the crochets, minims and quavers and all those other absurd characters. *I* am in charge of the *words*—the actions—and everything else . . .

SULLIVAN: But you have no right to be here today, sir.

GILBERT: I've as much right as you, sir.

SULLIVAN: Only with *my* permission! Music rehearsal days are *my* days.

CARTE: Yes, come on, Gilbert, old man, settle down.

GILBERT: Oh! I know you and Sullivan would like me to stay away altogether.

SULLIVAN: *(Appealing to* CARTE.) This is ridiculous. I'm trying to help these people to sing.

GILBERT: I'm surprised to find you here at all. I'm surprised that you were able to tear yourself away from your social engagements.

SULLIVAN: My private life has nothing to do with you, sir.

GILBERT: It has when it interferes with *my* plays.

SULLIVAN: Your plays. What do you mean?

GILBERT: It's no wonder you're always ill. The way you live.

SULLIVAN: That is my affair.

GILBERT: You make me ill.

SULLIVAN: I repeat. Nothing to do with you.

GILBERT: Well, there's one good thing for you, Sullivan, you have plenty of lady admirers to give you sympathy.

Whilst SULLIVAN *looks about to explode—*GILBERT *adds under his breath*

GILBERT: No wonder you're always ill. Vicious circle, if you ask me.

SULLIVAN: Carte! This man has completely destroyed the whole atmosphere for rehearsal. We cannot go on.

GILBERT: You don't need much of an excuse to give up work, do you?

CARTE: *(Rising and coming down.)* This isn't playing the game you know, Gilbert.

GILBERT: You keep out of it and do your sums—money is your game, Carte! Confine your thoughts to money!

CARTE: How dare you!

SULLIVAN: Oh, this is impossible. Get me my coat!

GILBERT: Stay here and earn *your* money.

SULLIVAN: You—don't need me! You don't need a musician. What you need is a barrel organ. . .

GILBERT: Yes—I've already got the monkey.

SULLIVAN: *(Beside himself with temper, hopping on the spot.)* What did you say, sir?

CARTE: I give up! *(He goes over to his desk.)*

SULLIVAN: *(Pointing across* CARTE *at* GILBERT.) Let me tell you, sir. I am entitled to some respect from *you!*

GILBERT: I'll give you respect when you behave worthily of respect.

Both men glare at each other. Light change. GILBERT, SULLIVAN *and* CARTE *freeze. Piano—"Lord High Executioner".*

GILBERT BEFORE SULLIVAN. SULLIVAN BEFORE GILBERT

JOE: On my right . . . Gilbert. Born eighteenth November eighteen thirty-six, seventeen Southampton Street, Strand. His grandfather's house. . .

JESSIE: His grandfather knew Dr. Johnson, Garrick and Reynolds. He is said to be descended from Sir Humphrey Gilbert.

ROSE: He is christened William. . .

JESSIE: Schwenck—Gilbert.

GROSSMITH: At the age of two, while on holiday in Italy, he is stolen from his nurse by brigands and taken to the mountains.

JESSIE: Pity he didn't stay there.

GERLADINE: But he is ransomed.

JESSIE: For twenty-five pounds.

JOE: On my left, six years later. Sullivan—born eight Bolwell Terrace.

Piano.

GILBERT: Lambeth. The unfashionable side of the river.

JOE: Please! Thirteenth May eighteen forty-two.

SULLIVAN: The year of Mendelssohn's *Spring Song.*

GROSSMITH: Sullivan makes discoveries for himself on the parlour piano.

JESSIE: And he's only eight.

GROSSMITH: He is christened Arthur. . .

SULLIVAN: Seymour Sullivan.

GILBERT: Initials, A.S.S

GERALDINE: Father—Irish. Clarinet player.

GILBERT: Mother looks after an organ grinder's monkey.

ALL: Shshsh!

JOE: Sullivan's father is bandmaster at Sandhurst.

Piano.

GERALDINE: He lets him play all the instruments in the band.

ROSE: He composes his first anthem.

JESSIE: And he's only eight.

GILBERT: Aah. . .

JOE: Gilbert at Great Ealing School.

GROSSMITH: *(As* SCHOOLMASTER.*)* If Gilbert took more pains with his lessons and less in fighting and writing plays, he might do well. . .

JESSIE: Sullivan is educated.

SULLIVAN: Privately.

GERLADINE: In Bayswater.

GROSSMITH: Dear Mrs. Sullivan. . .

JOE: The Reverand Thomas Helmore.

GERLADINE: Principal of the *Chapel Royal!*

GROSSMITH: *(As* HELMORE.*)* Dear Mrs. Sullivan, Arthur sang a very elaborate solo in church today. His expression brought tears to my eyes, but as I was immediately to enter the pulpit, I restrained myself.

JESSIE: Bless his little heart.

SULLIVAN: Dear Mother, the Prince Consort heard me sing, and gave me half a guinea. . .

GILBERT: Tip the monkey, ladies and gentlemen, and he'll turn the handle!

GILBERT *at University.*

GILBERT: Why do I have to study Shakespeare? I have nothing to learn from him. He's all gibberish. For instance, what does this mean? "I would as lief be thrust through a thicket hedge as cry pooh to a callow throstle."

GROSSMITH: *(As* TUTOR.*)* Obvious, obvious. A great lover of songsters rather than disturb a little warbler would prefer to go through a thorny hedge. But I cannot place the quotation.

GILBERT: I've just made it up.

Fanfare.

JOE: Eighteen fifty-six: Sullivan wins Mendelssohn Scholarship to the Royal Academy of Music.

JESSIE: And he's only seventeen.

JOE: Gilbert's first success as a writer.

GILBERT: *The Laughing Song.* A translation by. . .

Fanfare.

JOE: Sullivan wins the chance to study at the Leipzig Conservatoire.

JESSIE: The ladies flock to him.

ROSE: *(As* STUDENT*)* Oh, I am so impressed with Arthur. He is a natural courtier. When my turn comes to play I have no thoughts for anyone only how to impress this curly haired youth. . .

SULLIVAN: Dear Mother and Father, it's such fun conducting here at the Conservatoire. I can fancy Mother saying, "Bless his little heart. How it must be beating."

GILBERT: Bless his little heart.

JOE: Gilbert tries to join the army.

GILBERT: I want a commission to go and fight in the Crimean War.

GROSSMITH: *(As* ARMY OFFICER*)* The Crimean War's over, sonny.

GILBERT: Oh—well in that case. . .

JOE: Gilbert joins the Civil Service.

GILBERT: The worst bargain the Government ever made.

JOE: Gilbert receives a legacy of three hundred pounds.

GILBERT: Escapes from the Civil Service. . .

JOE: And becomes a Barrister at Law . . .

GILBERT: My lords. . .

JOE: In four years he earns—twenty-five pounds.

SULLIVAN *sits on the podium stool.*

GILBERT: The other night from cares exempt
I slept and what do you think I dreamt?
I dreamt that somehow I had come
To dwell in Topsy Turveydom.

JOE: Gilbert writes the *Bab Ballads!*

The Company, except for SULLIVAN, *gather around* GILBERT.

GROSSMITH: The Editor of *Fun* requests Mr. Gilbert to contribute one column of copy per week for the rest of his natural life.

GILBERT: I've jibe and joke
And quip and crank
For lowly folk
And men of rank
I ply my craft
And know no fear
But aim my shaft
At Prince or Peer
At Peer or Prince—at Prince or Peer
I aim my shaft and know no fear!
I've wisdom from the East and from the West
That's subject to no academic rule
You may find it in the jeering of a jest
Or distil it from the folly of a fool.
I can teach you with a quip if I've a mind
I can trick you into learning with a laugh;
Oh winnow all my folly folly folly and you'll find
A grain or two of truth among the chaff.
Oh winnow all my folly folly folly and you'll find
A grain or two of truth among the chaff.

GILBERT *sits at his desk.*

JOE: Sullivan soars to even greater success.

The Company move away to Sullivan.

JESSIE: Have you heard his *Tempest* at the Crystal Palace?

GROSSMITH: Magnificent. The audience went wild.

JESSIE: I always go along to St. Michael's to hear him play the organ; don't you?

GROSSMITH: No, but I have heard that Birmingham have asked him to compose something for their next festival.

SULLIVAN: *(Rising.)* I feel like a missionary spreading the light of music to those dark satanic cities of the north.

JESSIE: Did you hear he has composed a wedding march specially for Princess Alexandra?

ROSE: And a special song—*Bride of the North.*

GERALDINE: I have just heard Sullivan's Cello Concerto—splendid.

JESSIE: Ah, but you should hear his Symphony in E, my dear, out of this world.

GERALDINE: A new master of English music.

JESSIE: The first musician of our time.

SULLIVAN: There is so much to do for music if God would give me two days for every one in which to do it.

GILBERT: *(Rising.)* Excuse me!

All turn to GILBERT.

JOE: Gilbert sells his first play to Tom Robertson, the famous director.

GILBERT: Dulcimara or the little duck and the great quack; written in ten days—containing dances, sketches, mysteries, love potions, warriors, and lovesick maidens—a grand allegorical tableau of love's devices.

GROSSMITH: *(As* ROBERTSON*)* Hmmm, yes, this'll do. Thirty pounds.

GILBERT: Pounds. I don't deal in pounds. Make it guineas.

GROSSMITH: We don't deal in guineas.

GILBERT: Very well. Thank you, sir.

GROSSMITH: Here.

GILBERT: Yes.

GROSSMITH: Before you go, take a little bit of advice from an old stager. Never sell as good a piece as this for thirty pounds ever again.

JOE: From now on Gilbert has no time for the high and mighty.

GROSSMITH: Hey, you there.

GILBERT: Me?

GROSSMITH: Yes, you. Call me a cab.

GILBERT: If you insist. You are a fourwheeler, sir.

GROSSMITH: How dare you call me a fourwheeler!

GILBERT: Well, I could hardly call you handsome.

JOE: Romance. Gilbert marries the daughter of an Indian Army officer. Lucy Agnes . . .

GILBERT: Kitten.

JOE: Sullivan is pursued by Miss Rachel Scott Russell.

SULLIVAN *moves off the podium.*

JESSIE: *(As* RACHEL*)* Father built the Crystal Palace.

JOE: She encourages him—to write music.

JESSIE: (As RACHEL, *moving to* SULLIVAN.) Dear, Arthur, how is your Symphony in D? Do write it. It is the language you speak to me.

SULLIVAN: Yes, Rachel.

JESSIE: And dearest, I want you to write an opera—a grand, vigorous work.

SULLIVAN: Yes, Rachel—when I come back from Paris. By the by, what do you want from Paris?

JESSIE: Three pairs of cool cotton stockings. Blue is my favorite colour—and darling . . .

SULLIVAN: Yes, dearest?

JESSIE: I want you to write an octet—grander than Mendelssohn. Say you'll do it for me. Oh dearest, what will you do next?

GROSSMITH: I say, Sullivan.

JESSIE *moves away.*

JOE: Frederick Burnand, future editor of *Punch.*

GILBERT: And minor playwright.

GROSSMITH: (As BURNARD) Will you do me a personal favour?

SULLIVAN: Of course, old chap, if I can.

GROSSMITH: Good. Well, you couldn't knock together a bit of music for some private entertainment. No money, I'm afraid. Might be fun though.

SULLIVAN: What is it?

GROSSMITH: Well, it's a sort of burlesque operetta.

SULLIVAN: Oh?

GROSSMITH: Just for a bit of fun.

SULLIVAN: It might be rather a lark. What are you going to call it?

GROSSMITH: It's from *Box and Cox.* I thought we'd call it *Cox and Box.*

SULLIVAN: Give me a few days. Tell me the story.

GROSSMITH: It's about these two chaps who share the same room without knowing it. Their landlord is a military man.

Light change—taped applause.

GROSSMITH: I say, Sullivan. They're putting on *Cox and Box* at the Adelphi. It's a huge success. We must do another one.

GERALDINE: What is Sullivan thinking about squandering his genius in burlesque operetta?

ROSE: I thought he was supposed to be a serious composer.

JESSIE: Arthur, write me an oratorio.

GROSSMITH: They want to commission another burlesque operetta.

SULLIVAN: But there's this oratorio of mine.

GROSSMITH: There's money in this one.

SULLIVAN: Have you an idea?

GROSSMITH: Yes. I'm going to call it *The Contrabandista,* an adventure in the Spanish Mountains.

SULLIVAN: *The Contrabandista.*

Piano chord.

JOE: The box office takings do not cover the cost of the orchestra—and Sullivan returns to his oratorio.

JESSIE: I'm far prouder of the *Prodigal Son* than of anything. Everyone here is talking of your success.

SULLIVAN: So are all my friends. The Empress Eugenie, the Tzar and Tzarina of Russia. The Prince of Wales.

JESSIE: The *Prodigal Son* has made you the man of the hour.

SULLIVAN: I have had a letter from Queen Victoria.

ROSE: *(As* QUEEN VICTORIA) Dear Mr. Sullivan. We wish to receive a complete set of all your works—and we wish you to cast a critical eye over the compositions of our dear consort.

JOE: And now—

Fanfare.

JOE:—the first meeting.

All move away except GILBERT *and* SULLIVAN. CARTE *sits at his desk.*

SULLIVAN: Mr. Gilbert, I'm so pleased to meet you. I've heard so much about your work. In fact I do believe I have seen one of your plays. Ummm—*Robert the Devil*—it was very good, very good.

GILBERT: Very good, was it?

SULLIVAN: Yes, very good—very ummm—good.

GILBERT: Of course this is the point where I am supposed to say that one hears your music wherever one goes.

SULLIVAN: Oh, you are a lover of music?

GILBERT: I only know two tunes—one is "God Save The Queen", the other is "Pop goes the Weasel". Neither of them is yours, is it?

SULLIVAN: No. No.

GILBERT: Mmm—pity, thought one of them might have been. Still Sullivan since you're here perhaps you would consider . . .

Fanfare. The Company draw round again. JOE *holds up a poster* "Thespis".

GERALDINE: We don't think much of that.

ROSE: It's not what we're used to.

JESSIE: We expected pantomime, not a long, boring tale about a lot of seedy gods.

CARTE: *(Rising.)* It runs for only sixty-seven performances. *(He comes down.)*

Fanfare.

CARTE: Richard D'Oyly Cartre.

GERALDINE: Art lover.

GROSSMITH: Gourmet.

ROSE: Impresario.

CARTE: Now manager of the Royalty, Soho.

JESSIE: Some people call him Oily Carte.

JOE: He has a genius for backing outsiders.

SULLIVAN *sits on the podium.*

CARTE AND *TRIAL BY JURY*

CARTE: Mr. Gilbert. Carte.

GILBERT: Oh, yes?

CARTE: Very fortunate meeting you like this.

GILBERT: Fortunate for whom?

CARTE: For both of us, I trust.

GILBERT: Oh?

CARTE: Yes, I—er—find myself in a bit of predicament. I'm producing some entertainment at the Royalty in March, only a couple of weeks or so away—Offenbach's *La Perichole* . . .

GILBERT: Offenbach again?

CARTE *shrugs and smiles.*

CARTE: Yes, I know, I know, exactly, Mr. Gilbert. But even so, the programme is too short. I need another one-act musical piece. I'd like it to be a new one.

GILBERT: There must be many around.

CARTE: But not written by Gilbert and Sullivan . . .

GILBERT: Gilbert and . . . ?

CARTE: Sullivan.

GILBERT: Oh. Him! Well. I doubt if he'd be interested in doing any more work with me. He's too busy uplifting British music at present. They say he's working for a knighthood. He does have the knack of slipping a tune in the right quarter.

CARTE: Yes, but he is living beyond his means. He needs a lot of money to keep up with his contacts and his racing, cards, roulette—you can't lead that sort of life on the money you can earn for writing oratorio!

GILBERT: Come to the point, Carte.

CARTE: *(Directly.)* I want a script from you. Have you one?

GILBERT: I do happen to have one with me. *(Pulling out a tattered script.)* It is set in a court room.

CARTE: I was thinking of comic opera. Court rooms don't immediately suggest themselves as comic opera.

GILBERT: You've obviously never been in one of my courts . . .

CARTE: Come into my office. I'll get hold of Sullivan and you can read it to him.

CARTE *sits at his table.* GILBERT *and* SULLIVAN *take a chair each and sit either side of it.*

GILBERT: *(Bad-temperedly.) Trial by Jury,* a dramatic cantata in one act.

CARTE: *(Smiling, nodding as if already counting the audience.)* Very nice.

GILBERT: Scene. A court of justice. Barristers. Attorneys. Chorus . . .
Hark the hour of ten is sounding
Hearts with anxious fears are bounding
Hall of justice crowds surrounding
Breathing hope and fear . . .

Piano—"Hark the Hour of Ten is Sounding". Mime reading. SULLIVAN *laughs.*

GILBERT: Sir, this farce is clearly beneath both of us. Sir, unless you stop laughing and pay attention while I read, I must ask you to go outside. Sir, you may think this is amusing.

SULLIVAN: I do. I do. It's priceless. I can hear the tunes already.

CARTE: Then you'll do it?

SULLIVAN: Of course I'll do it. How long may I have?

CARTE: We can't rush matters of this nature. Shall we say a fortnight?

SULLIVAN: You shall have it in one week.

CARTE: Then, gentlemen—*(Shaking hands with both of them.)*—till we meet again—in court.

Music starts. The Company assemble. The Stage Hands set the Court unit "Trial by Jury" sequence:

TRIAL BY JURY

JUDGE: (GILBERT) When I, good friends, was called to the bar,
   I'd an appetite fresh and hearty,
But I was, as many young barristers are,
   An impecunious party.
But I soon got tired of third-class journeys,
   And dinners of bread and water;

So I fell in love with a rich attorney's
   Elderly, ugly daughter.

CHORUS: So he fell in love, etc.

JUDGE: The rich attorney, he jumped with joy,
   And replied to my fond professions:
"You shall reap the reward you pluck, my boy
   At the Bailey and Middlesex Sessions.
You'll soon get used to her looks," said he
   "And a very nice girl you'll find her!
She may very well pass for forty-three
   In the dusk, with a light behind her!"

CHORUS: She may very well, etc.

GILBERT *polkas with* JESSIE

CHORUS: In the dusk with a light behind her!

The Girls enter as a Chorus of Bridesmaids.

CHORUS: Comes the broken flower—
   Comes the cheated maid—
Though the tempest lower,
   Rain and cloud will fade!
Take, oh maid these posies:
   Though thy beauty rare
Shame and blushing roses,
   They are passing fair!

Repeat the last two lines.

CHORUS: Wear the flowers till they fade;
Happy be thy life, oh maid.
Happy Happy be thy life, oh maid.

JUDGE: That she is reeling
Is plain to see!

FOREMAN: (CARTE) If faint you're feeling
Recline on me!

JESSIE *falls sobbing on to the* FOREMAN'S *breast.*

PLAINTIFF: (ROSE) *(Feebly.)* I shall recover
If left alone.

ALL: *(Shaking their fists at Defendant.)* Oh, perjured lover,
Atone! Atone!

FOREMAN: Just like a father
I wish to be. *(Kissing her.)*

JUDGE: *(Approaching her.)* Or if you'd rather,
Recline on me!

JESSIE *jumps on to the Bench, sits down by the* JUDGE, *and falls sobbing on his breast.*

COUNSEL: (SULLIVAN) Oh! Fetch some water
From far Cologne!

ALL: For this sad slaughter
Atone! Atone!

JURY: *(Shaking their fists at the Defendant, all except* JOE.) Monster,
dread our fury . . .
There's the Judge, and there's the Jury!
Monster; monster, dread our fury!

USHER: (GROSSMITH) Silence in court!

JUDGE: Shhh.

COUNSEL: Don't you worry about a thing, my dear.

SONG

DEFENDANT: (JOE) Oh gentlemen, listen, I pray,
    Though I own that my heart has been ranging; Of nature
the laws I obey,
    For nature is constantly changing.
The moon in her phases is found,
    The time and the wind and the weather,

The months in succession come round,
   And you don't find two Mondays together.
Consider the moral, I pray,

   Nor bring a young fellow to sorrow,
Who loves this young lady today,
   And loves that young lady tomorrow.

Repeat last four lines.

BRIDESMAIDS: *(Rushing forward, and kneeling to the Jury.)* Consider the moral, etc.

ALL: But this I am willing to say,
   If it will appease her sorrow,
I'll marry this lady today,
   And I'll marry the other tomorrow!

Chorus repeat brackets, changing.

PLAINTIFF: *(Embracing him rapturously.)* I love him—I love him—with fervour unceasing
   I worship and madly adore;
My blind adoration is ever increasing,
   My loss I shall ever deplore.
Oh, see what a blessing, what love and caressing
   I've lost, and remember it, pray,
When you I'm addressing, are busy assessing
   The damages Edwin must pay!
   Yes, He must pay!

DEFENDANT: *(Repelling her furiously.)* I smoke like a furnace—
I'm always in liquor,
   A ruffian—a bully—a sot;
I'm sure I should thrash her, perhaps I should kick her;
   I am such a very bad lot!
I'm not prepossessing, as you may be guessing,
   She couldn't endure me a day;
Recall my professing, when you are assessing
   The damages Edwin must pay!

ROSE *clings to the* DEFENDANT *passionately; after a struggle, he throws her off into the arms of* COUNSEL.

ALL: Yes, he must pay.

RECITATIVE

JUDGE: The question, gentlemen—is one of liquor;
   You ask for guidance—this is my reply:
He says, when tipsy, he would thrash and kick her,
   Let's make him tipsy, gentlemen, and try!

COUNSEL: With all respect
I do object!

PLAINTIFF: I do object!

DEFENDANT: I don't object!

ALL: With all respect
We do object!

Refer to score for the DEFENDANT.

JUDGE: *(Tossing his books and papers about.)* All the legal furies
seize you!
No proposal seems to please you,
I can't sit up here all day,
I must shortly get away.
Barristers, and you, attorneys,
Get you on your homeward journeys;
Gentle, simple-minded Usher,
Get you, if you like, to Rus*sher*;
Put your briefs upon the shelf,
I will marry her myself!

He comes down from the Bench to the floor of the court. He embraces ROSE.

JUDGE: For I am a judge.

ALL: And a good judge too.

JUDGE: Yes, I am a judge.

ALL: And a good judge too!

JUDGE: Though homeward as you trudge,
You declare my law is fudge,
Yet of beauty I'm a judge.

ALL: And a good judge too!

JUDGE: Though defendant is a snob . . .

DEFENDANT: No, no, no!

ALL: And a great snob too! *(Repeat.)*
Though defendant is a snob
And a great snob too
He'll reward him from his fob
So we've settled with the job.
And a good job too.

Refer to score for JUDGE.

AFTER *TRIAL BY JURY*

Applause. GILBERT *and* SULLIVAN *return to their places.* GILBERT *stands at the podium,* CARTE *stands at his table. The Stage Hands strike the Court unit.*

CARTE: I do believe we have a success overnight.

HELEN: (GERALDINE) All London is whistling the tunes.

JOE: Helen Lenoir, D'Oyly Carte's secretary, later his second wife.

HELEN: The popular critics are raving about the show.

JOE: And Sullivan is dining out on his new-found success.

JOE *goes off and returns with a tray of champagne glasses, which he hands out. The drinkers cluster around* SULLIVAN.

JESSIE: Do tell me, Arthur, are you happy?

SULLIVAN: Am I happy? I don't know. I enjoyed the experience of putting on *Trial by Jury*, except for one slight altercation with Gilbert, who said at the end of one of the band rehearsals that he thought the music was "too loud"—tch—too loud!

SIR ALEXANDER COCKBURN: (GROSSMITH) I liked your music, Sullivan . . .

JOE: Sir Alexander Cockburn.

JESSIE: Lord Chief Justice.

SULLIVAN: Thank you, sir.

SIR ALEXANDER COCKBURN: It's all very clever and pretty, don't you know—but I shall never come and see it again, for fear of encouraging contempt of court—I'd get rid of that Gilbert if I were you!

JESSIE: I do agree, Rose dear, don't you?

The drinkers retire. CARTE *moves down to* GILBERT.

CARTE: Er, Gilbert!

GILBERT: *(At his desk, writing.)* Mmm?

CARTE: What would you say to an English Comic Opera Company to oust the French?

GILBERT: Sounds very grand. Where's the money coming from? I thought you were supposed to be reviving *Thespis*.

CARTE: The backers withdrew their money at the last moment.

GILBERT: Surprising how these capitalists quail at the words "money-down".

CARTE: The time is not right for *Thespis*. I want a new piece. A full-length opera.

GILBERT: Don't ask me. I'm sticking straight to plays at the moment.

CARTE: Look, I'll raise the money. I'll form a company. With a board of directors. I've got my eye on a theatre in Wych Street.

GILBERT: One—I want two hundred in advance . . .

CARTE: Pounds?

GILBERT: Guineas.

CARTE: All right.

GILBERT: Two—we choose our own company. Three, we control rehearsals. Four, we select the subject.

CARTE: I'll find Sullivan.

JOE: But Sullivan has been frightened off by his critics.

"MUSICAL STANDARD" JOURNALIST: (GERALDINE) It is to be gathered from the public prints that the versatile composer of *Light of the World* has turned all his attention to musical burlesque.

MUSIC CRITIC: (ROSE) *Trial by Jury,* as far as Sullivan is concerned, is a joke, but it has gone far enough, and Sullivan will now turn his attention to the more serious subject of English opera.

GROSSMITH: (*As* SPOKESMAN) Lady Lindsay has taken Sullivan to recover in Italy.

LADY LINDSAY (JESSIE) A few weeks by Lake Como will inspire you to greater things than comic cantatas.

CARTE: I wish to speak to Mr. Sullivan. Has he returned?

GROSSMITH: (*Shutting off* SULLIVAN.) Mr. Sullivan has returned from abroad.

ROSE: But he has gone up to Cambridge.

GERALDINE: He is now Principal of the New National College of Music.

JESSIE: Dr. Sullivan is so busy.

SULLIVAN: (*Writing.*) "Dearest Mum, Princess Louise is coming to my party tomorrow—so bring lots of roses. Blow the expense. P.S. The guests will include the Prince of Wales, the

Duchess of Westminister, the Lord Chief Justice . . . Mrs.
Ronalds . . . "

ROSE: Dr. Sullivan is there any truth in the rumour that you
may marry Mrs. Ronalds?

SULLIVAN *laughs.*

MRS. RONALDS: (GERALDINE) Arthur Sullivan has kindly at-
tended a few of my soirées—we are just—very good friends.

CARTE: Gilbert!

GILBERT: I know, I know, Carte. *(Writing.)* "Dear Sullivan, we
are going to write a new opera. We'll call it *The Sorcerer*—it's
about a modern magician who gives a whole village a love
potion—with hilarious results. There is a wickedly funny part
for your brother Fred—what do you say?"

Piano—"The Lost Chord".

GERALDINE: Dr. Sullivan is not at home.

GROSSMITH: Dr. Sullivan is at the bedside of his dying brother.

JESSIE: Dr. Sullivan's grief has inspired him to write *The Lost
Chord.*

ROSE: Dr. Sullivan is in mourning for his brother.

JOE: *The Lost Chord* is the most popular song in England.

The piano becomes livelier. ROSE, JESSIE, *and* GERALDINE *dance.*

SULLIVAN: Please, I ask you, I wrote *The Last Chord* in sorrow
as my brother lay dying—don't burlesque it—besides, it affects
the royalties. *(He sits.)*

The piano finishes. The girls exit.

GILBERT: Dear Sullivan. Dear *Dr.* Sullivan.

SULLIVAN: Thank you.

GILBERT: How are you getting on with the music for *The Sorcerer?* Can you help me to get the company together? Carte is badgering me.

CARTE: Gilbert, what is the delay with the new show?

GILBERT: We are trying to find the right cast.

CARTE: Hurry up.

GILBERT: You promised us full control.

CARTE: You already have that, but why aren't you moving faster?

GILBERT: I want to form the basis, now, for a permanent company—no so-called stars—no temperamental tenors— they can't act and they are more trouble than the rest of the company put together. I'd rather take on a bunch of amateurs and lick them into shape.

CARTE: Just hurry up.

SULLIVAN: Carte, Gilbert! Will you come down to Battersea. There's an entertainer there called Grossmith, ideal for our company, lecturing on Bombay.

GILBERT: Bombay!

CARTE: Bombay!

JOE *sets up a card table on which are a set of pictures for Grossmith's lecture.(*GROSSMITH *at the time was working as an "advertising quack")*

A poster: George Grossmith Jnr. entertains! New illuminated comic lecture—entitled "Bombay".

GILBERT, CARTE, SULLIVAN *take their places in front row of* GROSSMITH'S *audience.*

GROSSMITH: Finally. It is very dark at night in the city of Bombay. This is my view of Bombay by night taken with my

Kodachrome Viewfinder Master, purchased at Jidson's in the Strand . . . *(He holds up a completely black picture.* GILBERT *laughs very loudly which unnerves* GROSSMITH.*)* Details of any goods mentioned in the talk may be had on request. Oh, madam, madam—on your way out, you'll find that the manager of Jidson's has kindly set up a stall for your further interest in the lobby—there is so much to see in Bombay.

GILBERT: *(Approaching* GROSSMITH.*)* Grossmith, Sullivan tells me that you were once in the hands of the law.

JOE *strikes the card table.*

GROSSMITH: I beg your pardon. Oh, yes. That's right. I was a police reporter—Bow Street.

GILBERT: Miserable place—know it well. Now, I hear that Sullivan has auditioned you. We have just the part for you.

GROSSMITH: But, Mr. Gilbert, I'm not an opera singer. You need someone with a big strong voice for opera.

GILBERT: That's just what we don't want. This is comic opera.

GROSSMITH: Well, I never try to be funny—I mean: look funny—I don't make up. I never wear red noses . . .

GILBERT: No red noses for us. We are not looking for clowns. Carte! Take him away. Sign him up.

CARTE: *(Leading* GROSSMITH *over to his table.)* I can offer you six pounds per week.

GROSSMITH: Thank you.

GILBERT: *(Calling after* GROSSMITH.*)* Grossmith, rehearsals start on Monday.

GROSSMITH *signs the contract.* GILBERT *moves over to* SULLIVAN.

GROSSMITH: What's the matter, Sullivan? Your back bothering you again, you ought to go to bed at night instead of gadding around the clubs.

SULLIVAN: I've been talking to Carte. He says the Board don't like us employing people like George . . .

GILBERT: I know. But I want him.

SULLIVAN: They want more professional entertainers . . .

GILBERT: Bugger the Board!

SULLIVAN: Pardon.

GILBERT: Bugger 'em, Sullivan, bugger 'em.

SULLIVAN: Er, quite.

Piano—"John Wellington Wells".

GILBERT: We'll soon get George up to scratch. Get him started on *The Sorcerer.* You can work wonders on him.

GILBERT *exits.*

GROSSMITH: *(Singing his best, at half speed.)* My name is John Wellington Wells,
I'm a dealer in magic and spells,
In blessings and curses . . .

He is stopped by SULLIVAN. *The piano stops.*

SULLIVAN: *(Laughing.)* No—no—George, George. No, no, not like that. You see it says very *lively . . .* ,

The piano starts again.

GROSSMITH: I was being very lively . . .

SULLIVAN: Yes, but it means even more very lively. I mean, it's a patter song—goes like this . . . *(Singing.)* My name is John Wellington Wells.

THE SORCERER *(SONG: "MR. WELLS")*

SULLIVAN: My name is John Wellington Wells,

I'm a dealer in magic and spells,
   In blessings and curses
   And ever-filled purses,
In prophecies, witches, and knells.

If you want a proud foe to "make tracks"—
If you'd melt a rich uncle in wax—
   You've but to look in
   On the resident Djinn,
Number seventy, Simmery Axe!

GROSSMITH: We've a first rate assortment of magic;
   And for raising a posthumous shade
With effects that are comic or tragic,
   There's no cheaper house in the trade
Love-philtre—we've quantities of it;
   And for knowledge if any one burns,
We keep a very small prophet, a prophet
   Who brings us unbounded returns:

For he can prophesy
With a wink *of* his eye,
Peep with security
Into futurity,
Sum up your history,
Clear up a mystery,
Humour proclivity
For a nativity—for a nativity;
He has answers oracular—
Bogies spectacular
Tetrapods tragical
Mirrors so magical
Facts astronomical,
Solemn or comical,
And, if you want it, he
Makes a reduction on taking a quantity!
   Oh!
If anyone anything lacks,
He'll find it all ready in stacks,
   If he'll only look in

    On the resident Djinn,
    Number seventy, Simmery Axe!

JOE *brings in comic top hat and large bow. He puts the hat on* GROSSMITH'S *head and gives the bow to* SULLIVAN, *who puts it around* GROSSMITH'S *neck.*

SULLIVAN: Put this round your neck, like that.
Brighten you up a bit.

He can raise you hosts
    Of ghosts,

GROSSMITH: And that without reflectors;

SULLIVAN: And creepy things
With wings,

GROSSMITH: And gaunt and grisly spectres.

SULLIVAN: He can fill your crowds
Of shrouds,

GROSSMITH: And horrify you vastly;

SULLIVAN: He can rack your brains
With chains,

GROSSMITH: And gibberings grim and ghastly!
Then if you plan it, he

Changes organity,
With an urbanity,
Full of Satanity,
Vexes humanity
With an inanity
Fatal to vanity . . .

    Driving your foes to the verge of insanity!

Barring tautology,
In demonology,
'Lectro-biology,

Mystic nosology,
Spirit philology,
High-class astrology,
Such is his knowledge, he,
   Isn't the man to require an apology!
      Oh!
My name is John Wellington Wells, I'm a dealer in magic and
spells,
   In blessings and curses
   And ever-filled purses
In prophesies, witches, and knells.
If anyone anything lacks,
He'll find it all ready in stacks,
   If he'll only look in
   On the resident Djinn,
Number seventy, Simmery Axe!

SULLIVAN *and* GROSSMITH *exit.* GILBERT *enters in a hurry and*
starts to cross the stage.

CARTE: Ah, Gilbert. Where are you going to in such a hurry?

GILBERT: I'm rushing this new plot to Sullivan.

CARTE: He's not there.

GILBERT: Oh, not again.

CARTE: No. He's in Paris, recovering.

GILBERT: It's all that high living. I suppose he's doing platonic
tours of the city at night with Mary Rolands . . .

CARTE: No, I believe he has been very ill, and down . . .

GILBERT: Well, I'll post this off to him this might cheer him up.

CARTE: Before you do there is a slight problem.

GILBERT: What? Out with it.

CARTE: It's my board of directors.

GILBERT: Oh. Is it? I'm tired of that load of sharks. We've had nothing but trouble with them. They wanted to take *The Sorcerer* off after the first week.

CARTE: Box office takings were very low to begin with . . .

GILBERT: Of course they were. It was something new. You have to be prepared to lose at first with something new. But the word went around, and people started to come and see it. They soon changed their tune. "Will you write us another opera?" Up one minute down the next. Left to them they'd have killed us stone dead at the beginning. Now what's wrong with them?

CARTE: They want to cut your advance.

GILBERT: By how much?

CARTE: By half.

GILBERT: The devil they do. Let me get my hands . . .

CARTE: I know. I know.

GILBERT: And what did you say?

CARTE: Say?

GILBERT: Say, yes, say.

CARTE: I said it wouldn't do.

GILBERT: You're damn right it won't do! Now look here, Carte. They asked me to write a new book. Well, here it is. I stuck to my part of the bargain, they must keep to theirs. They're damn lucky after *The Sorcerer* I didn't ask for more money. Well, are you going to support me? If not now is the time to tell me.

SULLIVAN *enters.*

CARTE: Of course, of course, no question . . . Ah . . .

GILBERT: *(To* SULLIVAN) Carte's right. You don't look well. I've got just the thing for you! Now, Carte, you go and deal with that pack of sharks. Sullivan and I are off to Portsmouth.

CARTE *exits. A whistle is heard off.*

GILBERT AND SULLIVAN AT PORTSMOUTH

SULLIVAN: Portsmouth? Oh . . . yes . . .

GILBERT: Salt sea air, Sullivan. This is it. You should get plenty of this down you. Did I tell you that the blood of Sir Humphrey Gilbert runs in my veins?

SULLIVAN: *(Smiling with effort)* I believe you have mentioned it from time to time.

JOE *enters as a sailor.*

GILBERT: Ah, just look at the view, Sullivan. It's magnificient. I've never been so excited by an idea for a long time.

GILBERT *stops a sailor* (JOE).

GILBERT: Now tell me fine fellow, for you are a fine fellow . . .

SAILOR (JOE): Yes, Sir.

GILBERT: Leading seaman, aren't you?

SAILOR: Yessir.

GILBERT: I like the cut of your rig . . .

SAILOR: Thank you, sir.

GILBERT: I think he'll do very well, don't you, Sullivan . . . ?

The sailor is dismissed. JOE *exits. Piano—"H.M.S. Pinafore" music.*

GILBERT: I say, Sullivan, I've just had an idea . . . we'll have the uniforms made here—make them really authentic, eh? And don't you like my idea about the First Sea Lord who has never been to sea? Could only happen in England that. It has got to have a truly English feel about it this play. The joke of

English politics. The fact that we've made the First Sea Lord,
Sir Joseph Porter, a radical of the most pronounced type, will
allay any suspicions that it is W. H. Smith I'm getting at.
They'll never guess. *(With his tongue in his cheek, behind* SULLI-
VAN'S *back.)* We don't want to upset anybody in high places,
do we?

SULLIVAN *splutters.* GILBERT *claps him on the back.*

GILBERT: This sea air does wonders. Of course, I'm not getting
at anybody really. Just a bit of fun that's all. So long as we
make it good and funny, we'll be forgiven, don't worry. Oh
look, Sullivan, there's the *Victory.*

SULLIVAN: Oh yes.

GILBERT: Just imagine that on the back cloth—all the ropes
and the rigging—Spithead in the distance—all the sailors
waiting to welcome the First Sea Lord aboard. Can't you see
it all growing before your eyes . . .

The Company enter for the "Pinafore" sequence.

H.M.S PINAFORE

CHORUS: (ALL) We sail the ocean blue,
And our saucy's ship's a beauty;
We're sober men and true,
And attentive to our duty.
When the balls whistle free
O'er the bright blue sea,
We stand to our guns all day;
When at anchor we ride
On the Portsmouth tide,
We have plenty of time for play.

High
Ahoy! Ahoy!
Ahoy! Ahoy!
Low

The balls whistle free
O'er the bright blue sea

ALL: We stand to our guns to our guns all day
We sail the ocean blue,
And our saucy ship's a beauty.
We're sober men and true
And attentive to our duty.
Our saucy ship's a beauty.
We're attentive to our duty
We're sober men and true
We sail the ocean blue.

The GIRLS *represent Sir Joseph's Female Relatives.They dance round the stage.*

RELATIVES: (GIRLS) Gaily tripping,
Lightly skipping,
Flock the maidens to the shipping. *(Repeat the last three lines.)*

SAILORS: (MEN) Flags and guns and pennants dipping!
All the ladies love the shipping.

RELATIVES: Sailors sprightly
  Always rightly
Welcome ladies so politely

SAILORS: Ladies who can smile so brightly,
Sailors welcome most politely. *(Repeat. Refer to score.)*
We're smart and sober men
And quite devoid of fear
In all the Royal N
None are so smart as we are

LADIES: Gaily tripping
  Lightly skipping
Flock the maidens to the shipping. *(Repeat the last three lines.)*

SAILORS: Sailors sprightly
  Always rightly.
Welcome ladies so politely, so politely.

LADIES: Gaily tripping
  Lightly skipping,
Sailors always welcome ladies so politely. *(Repeat the last three lines.)*

ALL: *(counterpoint)* Ladies who can smile so brightly
Sailors welcome most politely, most politely.
  Gaily tripping
  Lightly skipping
Sailors always welcome ladies most politely.

CARTE *starts to sing immediately.*

CAPTAIN: (CARTE) Now give three cheers—
I'll lead the way.
Hip, hip, hip, hip—

ALL: Hurray! Hurray!
Hurray!

SONG

SIR JOSEPH (SULLIVAN) When I was a lad I served a term
As office boy to an attorney's firm.
I cleaned the windows and I swept the floor,
And I polished up the handle of the big front door.

CHORUS: He polished up the handle of the big front door.

SIR JOSEPH: I polished up that handle so carefullee
That now I am the Ruler of the Queen's Navee!

CHORUS: He polished, etc.

SIR JOSEPH: Now landsmen all, whoever you may be,
If you want to rise to the top of the tree,
If your soul isn't fettered to an office stool,
Be careful to be guided by this golden rule—

CHORUS: Be careful, etc.

SIR JOSEPH: Stick close to your desks and never go to sea
And you all may be Rulers of the Queen's Navee!

CHORUS: Stick close, etc.

GILBERT: Well, Carte. *Pinafore* seems to be very succesful.

CARTE: Yes, ladies and gentlemen, owing to the success of *Pinafore* I've decided to take you up-river on a boat trip picnic.

ALL: Cheers!

H.M.S. PINAFORE RECITATIVE

CAPTAIN: (CARTE) My gallant crew, good morning.

ALL: *(Saluting.)* Sir, good morning!

CAPTAIN: I hope you're all quite well.

ALL: *(As before.)* Quite well; and you, sir?

CAPTAIN: I am in reasonable health, and happy
To meet you all once more.

ALL: *(As before.)* You do us proud, sir!

SONG

CAPTAIN: I am the Captain of the *Pinafore*.

ALL: And a right good captain, too!

CAPTAIN: You're very, very good,
    And be it understood,
I command a right good crew,

ALL: We're very, very good
    And be it understood,
He commands a right good crew.

CAPTAIN: Though related to a peer,
I can hand, reef, and steer
    Or ship a selvagee;
I am never known to quail
At the fury of a gale,
    And I'm never, never sick at sea!

ALL: What, never?

CAPTAIN: No, never!

ALL: What, NEVER?

CAPTAIN: Well—hardly ever!

ALL: He's hardly ever sick at sea!
Then give three cheers, and one cheer more
For the hardy Captain of the *Pinafore!*
(Repeat the last two lines.)

CAPTAIN: You're exceedingly polite,
    And I think it only right
To return the compliment.

ALL: We're exceedingly polite,
    And he thinks it only right
To return the compliment.

CAPTAIN: Bad language or abuse
    I never, never use,
Whatever the emergency;
Though "BOTHER it" I may
Occasionally say,
I never use a big, big D—

ALL: What, never?

CAPTAIN: No, never!

ALL: What, NEVER?

CAPTAIN: Well, hardly ever!

ALL: Hardly ever swears a big, big D!
Then gives three cheers, and one cheer more,
For the well-bred Captain of the *Pinafore!*
Then give three cheers and one cheer more,
For the Captain of the *Pinafore!*

CARTE: I can't see the show going during this heat. *(He takes off the Captain's hat and jacket.)*

SULLIVAN: No, the summer was a bad time to open.

CARTE: I can't see us surviving the season.

GILBERT: Nonsense, Carte, don't worry.

CARTE: But Gilbert, the Board are very concerned.

GILBERT: As I keep saying. Bugger the Board, keep going.
(He takes the hat and jacket.)

CARTE *exits.* FIRST LORD, CAPTAIN *and* JOSEPHINE.

CAPTAIN: (GILBERT) Never mind the why and wherefore,
Love can level ranks, and therefore,
Though his lordship's station's mighty,
   Though stupendous be his brain,
Though her tastes are mean and flighty
   And her fortunes poor and plain.

CAPTAIN & SIR JOSEPH: Ring the merry bells on board-ship
   Rend the air with warbling wild,
For the union of (his/my) lordship
With a humble captain's child!

CAPTAIN: For a humble captain's daughter—

JOSEPHINE: (ROSE) For a gallant captain's daughter—

SIR JOSEPH: And a lord who rules the water—

JOSEPHINE: *(Aside.)* And a *tar* who ploughs the water—

ALL: Let the air with joy be laden,
   Rend with songs the air above,
For the union of a maiden
   With the man who owns her love!

Dance.

SIR JOSEPH: Never mind the why and wherefore
Love can level ranks, and therefore.

CARTE *enters.*

CARTE: Er—Gilbert . . .

GILBERT: Don't tell me. Trouble with the Board again.

CARTE: 'Fraid so.

GILBERT: What is it this time?

CARTE: They want to take it off.

GILBERT: *H.M.S. Pinafore?*

ALL:Oh no!

CARTE: I'm sorry.

GILBERT: The bloody fools!

CARTE: I know. I know.

GILBERT: But they can't take it off.

CARTE: The box office takings have been very low. It's this hot weather.

GILBERT: This is England. The hot weather can't last.

CARTE: If only we could survive these few weeks until the autumn. Believe me, Gilbert, I've done my best to make them see sense. I've told them also that if they do take it off it will be the death of English comic opera.

GILBERT: I give up. Can't you do something?

CARTE: Really, Gilbert. My head's on the block. If they take off *Pinafore,* I'm finished.

GILBERT *shrugs. "Well, that's it".*

SULLIVAN: I've got it.

GILBERT: *(Sarcastically.)* What shall we do, dedicate it to the Prince of Wales?

SULLILVAN: No—no—I mean it. I'm conducting at the promenade concert tonight. Leave it to me.

SULLIVAN goes to the podium to conduct. Placards are held up by the Stage Hands—PINAFORE MANIA: TOURS BEGIN: WHAT NEVER?: HARDLY EVER: 10,000 PIANO SCORES SOLD DAILY. The singers, including SULLIVAN, take their places.

SIR JOSEPH: Never mind the why and wherefore,
Love can level ranks and therefore,
Though your nautical relation *(Alluding to the CAPTAIN.)*
  In my set could scarcely pass—
Though you occupy a station
  In the lower middle class

Placards are held up.

CAPTAIN & SIR JOSEPH: Ring the merry bells on board-ship,
  Rend the air with warbling wild,
For the union of (his/my) lordship
With a humble captain's child!

CAPTAIN: For a humble captain's daughter—

JOSEPHINE: For a gallant captain's daughter—

SIR JOSEPH: And a lord who rules the water—

JOSPEHINE: *(Aside)* And a tar who ploughs the water!

ALL: Let the air with joy be laden,
  Rend with songs the air above,
For the union of a maiden
  With the man who owns her love!

Dance.

JOSEPHINE: Never mind the why and wherefore
Love can level ranks, and therefore

CARTE: Gilbert . . .

GILBERT glares at CARTE and can hardly speak.

CARTE: *(Shrugging, smiling.)* I know, I know.

GILBERT: You tell that damned and blasted Board that I have had a gut full of the whole lot of them . . .

SULLIVAN: And so have I. Let's buy them out . . .

GILBERT: You tell them that I'll come down personally and wring—their . . . What was that, Sullivan?

SULLIVAN: We can buy them out.

GILBERT: *(To* CARTE.) Are you with us?

CARTE: Right behind you.

GILBERT: Fix it up. Tell them we want them out in one month from today—that's when the contract expires. From then on they'll have no further claim on our work or on our properties.

CARTE: There may be reprisals, they are ruthless.

GILBERT: We'll handle any reprisals.

CARTE *turns way. The piano starts "Why and Wherefore".* ROSE/ JOSEPHINE *begins to sing "Never Mind".* CARTE *turns round carrying a travelling-bag.*

GILBERT: *(To* ROSE.) Be quiet. Where are you going, Carte? You can't run out on us now.

CARTE: I'm going to America. *Pinafore* is sweeping the States. It's a forest fire. Your words are on everyone's lips. On every street corner barrel-organs are churning out Sullivan's music.

SULLIVAN: Barrel-organs?

GILBERT: And we're not making a penny out of it. Can't you do something?

CARTE: I'm going to America myself. You take care of things whilst I'm away. On my return we'll fix up a new contract. But watch out for the Board, they threatened to stop performances.

JOSEPHINE: Never mind the why and wherefore,
Love can level ranks, and therefore
I admit the jurisdiction;
   Ably have you played your part;
You have carried firm conviction
   To my hesitating heart . . .

The song peters out, and the Lights fade to a Black-out. Sound of fight going on. JESSIE *comes forward with a candle.*

JESSIE: Ladies and gentlemen. We've had a slight brush with the Board who have tried to steal our properties. But we have routed them! The company is now ours, so on with the show!

Cheers. The Lights come up. The piano starts the intro of "Never mind the Why and Wherefore" but is interrupted by CARTE.

CARTE: I've fixed it! I've done it! I have done a deal with the Americans! We're going to put on the authorised version of *Pinafore* in New York. We're all going to America!

Cheers.

JOSEPHINE: *(Determined.)* Never mind the why and wherefore,
Love can level ranks, and therefore
I admit the jurisdiction
   Ably have you played your part;
You have carried firm conviction
   To my hesitating heart.

SULLIVAN: Very nice.

CAPTAIN & SIR JOSEPH: Ring the merry bells on board-ship,
   Rend the air with warbling wild,
For the union of (his/my) lordship
With a humble captain's child!

CAPTAIN: For a humble captain's daughter—

JOSEPHINE: *(ROSE)* For a gallant captain's daughter—

SIR JOSEPH: And a lord who rules the water—

JOSEPHINE: *(Aside)* And a tar who ploughs the water—
(Aloud) Let the air with joy be laden.

CAPTAIN & SIR JOSEPH: Ring the merry bells on board-ship

JOSEPHINE: For the union of a maiden—

CAPTAIN & SIR JOSEPH: For her union with his lordship.

ALL: Rend with songs the air above
For the man who owns her love!

The Company breaks up.

THE CONTRACT

The contract between GILBERT *and* SULLIVAN *and* CARTE *is to be signed.* CARTE *moves above the table,* GILBERT *and* SULLIVAN *to either side.* HELEN (GERALDINE) *joins them.*

CARTE: Well, gentlemen, we have rid ourselves of the Board. We are now our own masters. This is the contract I propose, from the date of the withdrawal of *H.M.S. Pinafore*. We shall each of us contribute trading capital—at present, let us say a thousand pounds each, now we shall review the situation periodically and adjust accordingly, but this will form the basis of the agreement.

GILBERT: It says here the profits will be divided *after* all expenses have been deducted.

CARTE: That is fair.

GILBERT: And who is to do the accounting?

CARTE: Helen will see that you are given a complete run down.

GILBERT: And we'll have to stick to this for five years?

CARTE: Yes.

GILBERT *signs*

CARTE: Thank you, Arthur.

GILBERT *passes the contract to* SULLIVAN, *who peruses the document.*

CARTE: Don't let this business hold us up, gentlemen. I mean here to protect us. We must move sharply now and take our own company to do *Pinafore* the way *we* want to do it in New York. We must take the fight right into the pirate's camp. They're robbing us of thousands a week . . .

GILBERT: Better still, we'll open our new show in New York. Much of the writing's finished. A lot of the music is ready. We'll rehearse it out there.

Piano—"Poor Wandering One"

CARTE: Splendid idea. You are far enough advanced to do that? Is it exciting?

GILBERT: Very exciting.

CARTE: Colourful?

GILBERT: Very colourful.

CARTE: Songs? Pleasant songs?

GILBERT: The music is . . . Superb . . .

CARTE: Come on, Arthur, sign.

SULLIVAN *turns to look towards* MABEL (ROSE), *who has approached.*

THE PIRATES OF PENZANCE

MABEL: (ROSE) For shame, for shame, for shame!

SONG

Poor wandering one!
Though thou has surely strayed,
  Take heart of grace,

Thy steps retrace,
Poor wandering one!
Poor wandering one!
If such poor love as mine
  Can help thee find
    True peace of mind—
Why, take it, it is thine!

GILBERT: Aren't you going to sign, Sullivan? To make everything legal between us.

SULLIVAN: Yes, and binding.

CARTE: We are not going to give offence in this opera, are we? We don't want another Pinafore-Smith!

GILBERT: Well, we do have this military chap in it, but—

Piano—"A Modern Major-General"

GILBERT: I don't think he'll give offence . . .

CARTE: What never?

GILBERT: Well . . . No, he won't give offence . . .

MAJOR-GENERAL (GROSSMITH) *replaces* MABEL.

SONG—MAJOR-GENERAL

GENERAL: (GROSSMITH) I am the very model of a modern Major-General,
I've information vegetable, animal and mineral,
I know the kings of England, and I quote the fights historical,
From Marathon to Waterloo, in order categorical—
I'm very well acquainted too with matters mathematical,
I understand equations, both the simple and quadratical,
About binomial theorem I'm teeming with a lot of news—

I haven't finished yet, what comes after that?

GILBERT: Hypotenuse.

GENERAL: Oh yes, quite right.
With many cheerful facts about the square of the hypotenuse
For my military knowledge, though I'm plucky and adventury,
Has only been brought down to the beginning of the century;
But still in matters vegetable, animal, and mineral,
I am the very model of a modern Major-General.

CARTE: Got a title for it yet , Gilbert?

GILBERT: We're going to fight the pirates with a play about pirates . . . so we'll call it the *Pirates* . . .

CARTE: Just the *Pirates?*

GILBERT: No—let me see. We'll call it the—Pirates of Cornwall . . . no . . . of . . . Oh, I don't know . . .

The piano starts.

GILBERT: Ah . . . I've got it—Pirates of Penzance.

CARTE: Ah! The Pirates of Penzance. That's got a nice ring to it.

JOE *enters, dressed as an odd-looking pirate.*

SONG—PIRATE KING

Oh, better far to live and die
Under the brave black flag I fly,
Than play a sanctimonious part,
With a pirate head and a pirate heart.
Away to the cheating world go you,
Where pirates are all well-to-do;
But I'll be true to the song I sing,
And live and die a Pirate King.
   For I am a Pirate King.

   And it is, it is a glorious thing
   To be a Pirate King!
(Repeat the last two lines.)
   Hurrah for the Pirate King.

The Stage Hands bring on luggage and other impedimenta for a journey and start preparations.

GILBERT: That's it, let's get moving.

CARTE: It will be a challenge in America. But if we pull it off . . .

GILBERT: They started this fight. They threw down the challenge. They're going to end up with bloody noses . . .

CARTE: It's not going to be easy, though. That's why we need to be united. Arthur, you still haven't signed.

GILBERT: What is the matter with you, Sullivan. Cold feet?

CARTE: Now, don't cause a fuss. *(Soothingly.)* Now, Arthur, old chap, just sign and let us get this business out of the way.

SULLIVAN: Five years is a long time for a serious composer to commit himself to comic opera.

GILBERT: Look, don't underrate these comic operas. They are good pieces of work, and what is more they've already earned you far more money than any of your so-called serious stuff, so don't throw stones at them. You'll not catch Carte throwing stones. Will you?

CARTE: Me? No. Never . . .

GILBERT: What never?

CARTE: Well, not yet.

Piano—"Tarantara!". SULLIVAN *slowly picks up his pen.*

CARTE: Come on, Arthur, sign. I'll have a word with Gilbert. But America will put him in his place. It is you they are waiting to meet out there. Just sign there. No more petty squabbling. There is money to be earned. And a common enemy to fight. We're going to *America!*

All the bags are packed ready.

JOE: Don't forget your baton.

The Men pick up various bags. The Girls line up with them, ready to march.

SONG—SERGEANT

SERGEANT: (CARTE) When the foreman bares his steel,
  Tarantara! tarantara!
We uncomfortable feel,
  Tarantara!
And we find the wisest thing,
  Tarantara! tarantara!
Is to slap our chests and sing
  Tarantara!
For when threatened with emeutes,
  Tarantara! tarantara!
And your heart is in your boots,
  Tarantara!
There is nothing brings it round
Like the trumpet's martial sound,
(Repeat line.)
  Tarantara! tarantara!
Tarantara-ra-ra-ra-ra!

ALL: Tarantara-ra-ra-ra-ra! *(Refer to score.)*

MABEL: (ROSE) Go, ye heroes, go to glory,
Though you die in combat gory,
Ye shall live in song and story.
  Go to immortality!
Go to death, and go to slaughter;
Die, and every Cornish daughter
With her tears your grave shall water.
Go, ye heroes, go and die!
  Go, ye heroes, go and die!

GIRLS: Go, ye heroes, go and die!

POLICE: (GILBERT) Though to us it's evident,

Tarantara! tarantara!
These attentions are well meant,
  Tarantara!
Such expressions don't appear,
  Tarantara, tarantara!
Calculated men to cheer,
  Tarantara!
Who are going to meet their fate
In a highly nervous state,
  Tarantara! Tarantara! Tarantara!
Still to us it's evident
These attentions are well meant.
  Tarantara! Tarantara! Tarantara!

EDITH: (JESSIE) Go and do your best endeavour,
And before all links we sever,
We will say farewell for ever.
  Go to glory and the grave! Go to glory and the grave!

GIRLS: For your foes are fierce and ruthless,
Young and tender, old and toothless,
  All in vain their mercy crave.

SERGEANT: (SULLIVAN) We observe too great a stress,
On the risks that on us press,
And of reference a lack
To our chance of coming back.
Still, perhaps it would be wise
Not to carp or criticize,
For its very evident
These attentions are well meant.

MEN: Yes it's very evident
These attentions are well meant
Evident, yes well meant,
Evident, ah yes, well meant.

SONG—SERGEANT

SERGEANT: (CARTE) When the foeman bares his steel,
  Tarantara! tarantara!

We uncomfortable feel,
   Tarantara!
And we find the wisest thing,
   Tarantara! tarantara!
Is to slap our chests and sing
   Tarantara!
For when threatened with émeutes,
   Tarantara! tarantara!
And your heart is in your boots,
   Tarantara!
There is nothing brings it round,
Like the trumpet's martial sound,
(Repeat.)
   Tarantara! tarantara!
   Tarantara-ra-ra-ra-ra!

ALL: Tarantara-ra-ra-ra-ra! *(See score.)*

MABEL: Go, ye heroes, go to glory,
Though ye die in combat gory,
Ye shall live in song and story
   Go to immortality!
Go to death, and go to slaughter;
Die, and every Cornish daughter
With her tears your grave shall water.
Go, ye heroes, go to immortality

GIRLS: Go, ye heroes, go and die!
Go, ye heroes, go to immortality
Though ye die in combat gory
Ye shall live in song and story.

MABEL: Go to immortality.

EDITH: Away, away!

POLICE: *(Without moving.)* Yes, yes, we go.

EDITH: These pirates slay.

POLICE: Tarantara!

EDITH: Then do not stay,

POLICE: Tarantara!

EDITH: Then why this delay?

POLICE: All right—we go.
Yes, forward on the foe!
(Repeat—see score.)

EDITH: Yes, but you don't go!

POLICE: We go, we go!
Yes, forward on the foe!
(Repeat)

EDITH: Yes, but you don't go!
(See score)

POLICE: We go!

GIRLS: At last they really go.

The Men march off, as—

the Curtain falls.

ACT TWO

The Company are discovered performing an extract from "Patience".
The lovesick maidens (JESSIE, ROSE, and GERALDINE) are fawning
over BUNTHORNE (GILBERT).

PATIENCE

GIRLS: Twenty love-sick maidens we,
Love-sick all against our will.
Twenty years hence we shall be—
Twenty love-sick maidens still.

Enter the chorus of Dragoons, marching briskly.

MEN: The soldiers of our Queen
  Are linked in friendly tether;
Upon the battle scene
  They fight the foe together.
There every mother's son
  Prepared to fight and fall is;
The enemy of one
  The enemy of all is!
(Repeat the last two lines.)

COLONEL: (SULLIVAN) Stand at ease!

SONG—COLONEL

When I first put this uniform on,
I said, as I looked in the glass,
  "It's one to a million
  That any civilian
My figure and form will surpass.

Gold lace has a charm for the fair,
And I've plenty of that, and to spare,
  While a lover's professions,
  When uttered in Hessians,
Are eloquent everywhere!"
  A fact that I counted upon,
  When I first put this uniform on!

CHORUS OF DRAGOONS

MEN: By a simple coincidence, few
  Could ever have counted upon,
The same thing occured to me, too,
  When I first put this uniform on!

COLONEL: I said, when I first put it on,
"It is plain to the veriest dunce,
  That every beauty
  Will feel it her duty
To yield to its glamour at once.
They will see that I'm freely gold-laced
In a uniform handsome and chaste"—
  But the peripatetics
  Of long-haired aesthetics
Are very much more to their taste—
  Which I never counted upon,
  When I first put this uniform on!

MEN: By a simple coincidence, few
  Could have ever reckoned upon,
I didn't anticipate that,
  When I first put this uniform on!

The Men exit. BUNTHORNE *dismisses the* GIRLS.

GIRLS: Oh no! Not that.

BUNTHORNE *is adamant and strikes a pose. The girls exit.*

BUNTHORNE: (GILBERT) Am I alone and unobserved? I am.
Then let me own. I'm an aesthetic sham.

SONG

If you're anxious for to shine in the high
  aesthetic line as a man of culture rare,
You must get up all the germs of the transcendental
  terms, and plant them everywhere.
You must lie upon the daisies and discourse in novel
  phrases of your complicated state of mind,
The meaning doesn't matter if it's only idle
  chatter of a transcendental kind.
  And every one will say,
    As you walk your mystic way,
"If this young man expresses himself in terms
  too deep for *me*,
Why, what a very singularly deep young man this
  deep young man must be!"
Then a sentimental passion of a vegetable fashion
  must excite your languid spleen,
An attachment à la Plato for a bashful young
  potato, or a not-too French french bean!
Though The Philistines may jostle, you will rank
  as an apostle in the high aesthetic band,
If you walk down Piccadilly with a poppy or a lily
  in your mediaeval hand.
  And every one will say,
    As you walk your flowery way,
"If he's content with a vegetable love which would
  certainly not suit me,
Why, what a most particularly pure young man
  this pure young man must be!"

GILBERT *exits.* JOE *enters, followed by all except* GILBERT. *They
gather round* CARTE'S *table.*

JOE: Summer eighteen eighty-one. Richard D'Oyly is basking
in the financial and aesthetic glow of *Patience,* and momentarily
secure in the knowledge that his two protagonists are not yet
at each other's throats, he holds a press conference.

REPORTER: (GERALDINE) Of course, Mr. Carte, in *Patience*, Gilbert and Sullivan are attacking the Art world.

CARTE: In satirizing the excesses of the so-called aesthetes the authors of *Patience* have not desired to cast ridicule on the true aesthetic spirit, but only to attack unmanly oddities which masquerade in its likeness.

REPORTER: (GROSSMITH) Come on, Mr. Carte, they're knocking Oscar Wilde, aren't they?

CARTE: Not at all. Mr. Gilbert has every respect for Mr. Wilde both as an artist and as a personality. It is the imitators of Mr. Wilde that he is attacking.

REPORTER: (ROSE) Has Oscar Wilde made any comments on *Patience?*

CARTE: He has seen it twice and he laughed a good deal. In fact, he told me personally how much he enjoyed it. And to show that there is no ill will between us, he is shortly to do a lecture tour of the United States for me . . .

REPORTER: (JESSIE) Oh. You are sending him out, before the touring company, as an advertisement.

CARTE: Well, I could hire sandwich-board men with uncut hair much more cheaply.

REPORTER: (JOE) Mr. Carte, there are rumours of a new project in the air.

CARTE: Yes, I intend to house my new operettas . . .

REPORTERS: (ALL) In a new theatre?

CARTE: On the site of the old Savoy Palace. It will seat over one thousand and two hundred persons. And instead of the usual foul-smelling gas lamps, I intend to install a new electric light . . .

JOE *exits and re-enters immediately with an electric light bulb on a cushion, and a hammer.*

REPORTERS: (ALL) Electric light?

GILBERT *enters.*

CARTE: I just happen to have a bulb here. *(He holds up the bulb and hammer.)* Much cleaner. Much brighter. And certainly much safer. I will demonstrate.

GILBERT: Hold on there. Are you personally financing this venture?

All but GILBERT *and* CARTE *exit.*

CARTE: Yes.

GILBERT: By our agreement we share profits and costs. Electricity is going to put the costs up.

CARTE: Yes, but the box office takings will be much greater. Believe me, Gilbert, I know what I am doing. Supposing we draw up a new agreement whereby we each of us pay four thousand pounds per year rent.

GILBERT: You mean you as partner will pay yourself as landlord one-third of the rent?

CARTE: Yes.

GILBERT: You've made a very good investment there, Carte, you can't lose, but I don't think it will be much good to Sullivan and I . . .

CARTE: Gilbert, you are already earning over ten thousand per year. That's more than the Prime Minister gets.

GILBERT: I bring more pleasure to people than the Prime Minister does.

SULLIVAN *enters and sits on his podium, smoking cigarette in long holder, glass of wine in hand.*

CARTE: And what about that *new* luxury palace you are building in Kensington—with all those bathrooms . . . ?

GILBERT: At least I don't gamble it all away like Sullivan—this won't do, Carte. I'll ring Sullivan on my *new* telephone.

A golden light comes up on SULLIVAN. *Ladies cluster round him offering chocolates, mopping his brow, etc.*

SULLIVAN: *(In the sun.)* You can't.

GILBERT: Why not?

SULLIVAN: I'm not there.

GILBERT: Where are you?

SULLIVAN: I'm cruising in the Baltic with Alfie.

GILBERT: Alfie? Alfie who?

SULLIVAN: Duke of Edinburgh.

GILBERT: I might have known.

SULLIVAN: Oh, by the by, the King of Denmark looked after us frightfuly well.

GILBERT: Really? I'm so glad.

SULLIVAN: And I have never tasted food like the Tsar gave us.

GILBERT: Fascinating.

SULLIVAN: Oh, and when I met Prince Wilhelm, he bowed and sang, "He polished op ze hondle on ze big front door". We all roared, it was too funny.

GILBERT: What a riot. Perhaps after your cruise, you wouldn't mind sparing some thought to business, Carte is opening a new theatre . . .

SULLIVAN: I know, I know.

GILBERT: With electric lamps burning all over the place.

SULLIVAN: Very bright and cheerful.

GILBERT: He's going to charge us four thousand pounds per year rent.

SULLIVAN: Mmmm. Well, mmmm . . . ladies!

GILBERT: And I have the plot of our new comic opera ready.

SULLIVAN: Aha . . . in that case . . .

CARTE: Splendid.

The golden light fades. The Ladies exit. GILBERT *and* SULLIVAN *stand on either side of* CARTE.

GILBERT: —So, you see, the old crone swallows the lozenge . . .

SULLIVAN: Excuse me. Pardon me . . . Swallows?

CARTE: A lozenge, Sullivan.

SULLIVAN: Ahh. Continue.

GILBERT: She swallows a lozenge and right away becomes a ravishing beauty, young, sweet, pretty, hmmmph?

SULLIVAN: Hmmmmm.

CARTE: Sounds very nice—good.

GILBERT: Now the young woman swallows a lozenge . . .

SULLIVAN: And she becomes an old woman.

GILBERT: That's it, you've got it.

SULLIVAN: And the handsome hero, you mentioned, he swallows a a lozenge—

CARTE: *(Excitedly)* —and he becomes an old man.

GILBERT: Exactly . . .

CARTE: And you have an old man who swallows this—this—

SULLIVAN: —lozenge—

CARTE: —lozenge—and he becomes—

SULLIVAN: —a young man–and you have a good man and he swallows this lozenge and he becomes evil—and you have an evil man who becomes good—a cat who becomes a dog—and so on and so on—all swallowing lozenges . . .

CARTE: Yes, yes.

GILBERT: Yes, yes.

SULLIVAN: And everything goes topsy-turvy again.

GILBERT: Yes. Do you like it?

SULLIVAN: No.

GILBERT: Why not?

SULLIVAN: It's a lot of nonsense. What we want is realism.

CARTE: Yes, yes. Lozenges are all very well, Gilbert. But we do want realism.

GILBERT: Carte, what are you blathering about? Just because Sullivan has realism on the brain—not that I think he knows what it means—do you have to parrot him? "What we want is realism." Do you think these plots grow on trees?

CARTE: No, but I just think that we could fill the bill nicely with something a little more realistic.

GILBERT: Do you realize that while you have been gadding about the Continent, I have been sweating blood to get this plot right. My gout's ten times worse. I have not been to bed for a fortnight. And God knows how many more sleepless nights this is going to cost me.

CARTE: (Going to sit at his table.) Oh, but you'll get it, Gilbert old man. You always do.

GILBERT sits at his desk.

SULLIVAN: Look. Let me know when you come up with something. I must dash now, Carte. So much work has piled up while I've been away. Do you mind if I use your telephone? (He does.) Mayfair two-six-oh, please ... Mrs. Ronalds, please ... Hello, Mary ...

GILBERT: Hello, Mary.

SULLIVAN: Sorry to have kept you ... I'm on my way now. 'Bye ... (He replaces the receiver.) Cheer up, Gilbert. Try and get some sleep.

GROSSMITH enters.

GILBERT: Sleep—sleep! (He leans over the desk and tries to sleep.)

Piano.

NIGHTMARE SONG

LORD CHANCELLOR: (GROSSMITH) When you're lying awake
with a dismal headache,
  and repose is tabooed by anxiety
I conceive you may use any language you choose to indulge
  in without impropriety
For your brain is on fire—the bedclothes conspire
  of usual slumber to plunder you.
First your counterpane goes, and uncovers your toes,
  and your sheet slips demurely from under you.
Then the blanketing tickles—you feel like mixed pickles—
  so terribly sharp is the pricking
And you're hot and you're cross, and you tumble and
  toss till there's nothing twixt you and the ticking
Then the bedclothes all creep to the ground in a heap,
  and you pick 'em all up in a tangle
Next your pillow resigns and politely declines to remain
  at its usual angle.
Well you get some repose in the form of a doze, with
  hot eyeballs and head ever aching.
But your slumbering teems with such horrible dreams
  that you'd very much better be waking
For you dream you are crossing the Channel and tossing
  about in a Steamer from Harwich
Which is something between a large bathing machine and
  a very small second-class carriage
And you're giving a treat (penny ice and cold meat) to
  a party of friends and relations.
They're a ravenous horde— and they all come on board to
  Sloan Square and South Kensington Stations.
And bound on that journey you find your attorney (who
  started that morning from Devon)
He's a bit undersized and you don't feel surprised
  when he tells you he's only eleven.
Well you're driving like mad with this singular lad
  by the by the ship's now a four-wheeler

And you are playing round games and he calls you bad
    names when you tell him that ties pays the dealer
But this you can't stand, so you throw up your hand,
    and you find you're as cold as an icicle
In your shirt and your socks (the black silk with
    gold clocks) crossing Salisbury Plain on a bicycle
And he and his crew are on bicycles too—which they've
    somehow or other invested in—
And he's telling the tars all the particulars of a
    company he's interested in
It's a scheme of devices to get at low prices all goods from
    cough mixtures to cables
(Which tickled the sailors) by treating retailers
    as though they were all vegetables
You get a good spadesman to plant a small tradesman
    (first take off his boots with a boot tree)
And his legs will take root, and his fingers will shoot,
    and they'll blossom and bud like a fruit tree—
From the greengrocer tree you get grapes and green pea,
    cauliflower, pineapple and cranberries
While the pastrycook plant cherry brandy will grant
    apple puffs and three corners and Banbury's.
The shares are a penny, and ever so many are taken by
    Rothschild and Baring
And just as a few are allotted to you, you awake with a
    shudder despairing—
You're a regular wreck, with a crick in your neck,
and no wonder you snore, for your head's on the floor,
and you've needles and pins from your soles to your
shins, and your flesh is a-creep, for your left leg's
asleep and you've cramp in your toes, and a fly in your
nose, and some fluff in your lung, and a feverish tongue,
and a thirst that's intense, and a general sense that you
haven't been sleeping in clover;
    But the darkness has passsed and it's daylight at last,
and the night has been long—ditto ditto my song—
and thank goodness they're both of them over.

LORD CHANCELLOR *taps* GILBERT *on the shoulder to wake him, and then exists.* GILBERT *slams his desk.*

GILBERT: I've got it. I've got it all worked out. It's about this chap who's a fairy—but only from the waist up. He goes into Parliament and runs amok in the House of Lords. There's a chorus of Peers and a chorus of fairies—Lord Chancellor— ideal for Grossmith. *(He writes feverishly.)*

GROSSMITH *enters and crosses behind* GILBERT

CARTE *sits at his table.* SULLIVAN *and* GROSSMITH *move to it.*

GROSSMITH: Mr. Carte, Mr. Sullivan.

CARTE: Just a minute, George.

GROSSMITH: Mr. Sullivan, I'm still very worried about the Nightmare song.

SULLIVAN: Don't worry, George, just do it as you did it in rehearsal. On a first night nobody's going to know if you get the words right or not!

GROSSMITH: Mr. Gilbert will.

SULLIVAN: He won't be in.

GROSSMITH: No, no, he won't. No, he never is on a first night. Why's that?

SULLIVAN: He can't face them.

GROSSMITH: What? Mr. Gilbert?

CARTE: He's more nervous than you are. He spends his time walking up and down the Embankment, or at his Club until it is time for him to come and take his curtain call . . .

CARTE: Is everything all right now, George?

GROSSMITH: Yes thank you, Mr. Carte. I feel a lot better now. Good luck, Mr. Sullivan. *(He starts to go.)*

SULLIVAN: Good luck, George.

CARTE *waves*. GROSSMITH *exits*.

CARTE: Now then, Arthur, what is it? You look terrible.

SULLIVAN: I feel terrible. *(He sits by the table.)* I ache and I'm in pain and I can't get anything to soothe it.

CARTE: I was very sorry to hear about your mother.

SULLIVAN: It is not only that. Look, Carte, can I tell you something very confidential?

CARTE: Yes.

SULLIVAN: Don't tell anybody, not even Gilbert. Especially Gilbert. Carte, I am financially ruined, cleaned out.

CARTE: Gambling?

SULLIVAN: No. Not at the tables, anyhow. *(Producing a paper.)* Look, this arrived just as I was leaving for the theatre this evening . . .

CARTE: *(Taking the paper and reading.)* Cooper and Hall . . .

SULLIVAN: My brokers. They've gone bankrupt. Every penny I had in the world was with them. It has all gone.

CARTE: But surely you must have other resources.

SULLIVAN: No—nothing. I can't take much more, Carte. I feel old and tired and on top of everything there's Gilbert. I'm beginning to dread working with him. He deliberately refuses to feed me the kind of material I desperately need. Carte, when I go through crises like this, I feel terrified, I suddenly realize how short life is. Carte, I must achieve something before I die . . .

CARTE: You shall, I'll help you all I can. I cannot say more than that at present. I do realize how you must be feeling . . .

SULLIVAN: Do you? I wonder. *(Rising.)* I'm sorry, I didn't mean that, it's just that I have to pay heavily for my pleasures. And when troubles come—I'd like to escape from it all.

JESSIE *enters, followed by* SYBIL *and* GERALDINE. JOE *follows with jacket and bearskin for* SULLIVAN.

FAIRY QUEEN (JESSIE): Private Willis.

Piano

SENTRY: (SULLIVAN) Ma'am.

QUEEN: To save my life it is necessary that I marry at once. How would you like to be a Fairy Guardsman?

SENTRY: Well, ma'am, I don' think much of a British soldier who wouldn't ill-convenience himself to save a female in distress.

QUEEN: You are a brave fellow. You are a fairy from this moment! And how say you, my lords? Will you join our ranks?

LORD MOUNT: (GILBERT) Well, now that the Peers are to be recruited from persons of intelligence I don't see what use we are down here, do you, Tolloller?

TOLLOLLER: (CARTE) None whatsoever.

QUEEN: Good! Then away we go to Fairyland.
   Soon as we may off and away.

IOLANTHE

SONG

GIRLS: Soon as we may,
   Off and away!
We'll commence our journey airy—
   Happy are we—
   As you can see,
Everyone is now fairy!

ALL: Every, every, every, every, everyone is now a fairy!

IOLANTHE: (ROSE) Though as a general rule we know

QUEEN: Two strings go to every bow,

PHYL: (GERALDINE) Make up your minds that grief 'twill bring.
  If you've two beaux to every string.

LORD CHANCELLOR: Up in the sky,
  Ever so high,
Pleasures come in endless series;
  We will arrange
  Happy exchange—
House of Peers to House of Peris!

ALL: Peris, Peris, Peris
House of Peers to House of Peris!

LORD CHANCELLOR & MOUNT TOLLOLLER: *(Together)*
Up in the air, sky-high, sky-high,
Free from Wards in Chancery,
(I/He) will be surely happier, for
(I'm/He) such a susceptible Chancellor.
(Repeat "Up in the air . . . " until interupted.)

CRITIC 1: (JESSIE) Where is this topsy-turveydom going to end?

CRITIC 2: (GROSSMITH) I'd rather watch a Punch and Judy
show.

CRITIC 1: Doesn't come within a mile of *Pinafore.*

JOE *enters with a tray of champagne glasses which he hands round.*

CRITIC 1: Sullivan is a masterly musician, but he's sacrificing
himself to Gilbert . . .

JOE: Thirteenth May eighteen eighty-three. Dr. Sullivan is
forty-one today. He is giving a cocktail party. Everyone who
is anyone is here—the leading critics—Prince of Wales—Mrs.
Ronalds . . . Mr. Carte. And even Mr. Gilbert is enjoying himself.

AMERICAN WOMAN: (ROSE) *(having trailed* GILBERT*)* Wonderful
man, your Dr. Sullivan.

GILBERT: Yes, wonderful.

AMERICAN WOMAN: His music is so very popular all over the
United States. You know, Mr. Ahhh . . .

GILBERT: Gilbert.

AMERICAN WOMAN: Oh yes, Mr. Gilbert, yes. You're so very lucky to have the privilege of knowing and working with him.

GILBERT: Yes, It's very sacrificial of him to allow it to happen.

AMERICAN WOMAN: Pardon me?

GILBERT: It is always an education working with a great composer.

AMERICAN WOMAN: I'm sure it is, I am sure it is. You know, in America we have nothing like your European composers— we just love your European composers. Have you met many of them?

GILBERT: Oh, one comes across 'em, you know, in odd places.

AMERICN WOMAN: Oh, you're so lucky—Mr. Gilbey . . .

GILBERT: Gilbert.

AMERICAN WOMAN: Mr. Gilbert, Mr. Baych, Joe-Ann Sebaystian Baych, he is still composing?

GILBERT: No, madam, I think not, at present I believe he is by way of decomposing . . .

A WAITER: (JOE) Ladies and gentlemen, it is now nine-thirty . . .

SULLIVAN: I want you all to come and listen to my telephone.

All except GILBERT *show delight.* JOE *collects the glasses and exits.*

MRS. RONALDS: (GERALDINE) Oh, Mr. Gilbert, you musn't miss our surprise, we are just about to go through and listen into the telephone! To hear the second act of *Iolanthe* right from the stage of the Savoy . . .

GILBERT: It's hardly a surprise for me, I am able to do that whenever I please.

MRS. RONALDS: But it will be a thrill for my friends, don't you think?

GILBERT: Possibly, Mrs. Ronalds, possibly, but I'd find it even more thrilling if they were to buy tickets for tomorrow night's performance. Good night, Mrs. Ronalds.

GILBERT *exits.* JOE *enters with a note on a salver for* SULLIVAN.

SULLIVAN: Mary, the Prince of Wales has just congratulated me, but I do not know for what.

MRS. RONALDS: Well may I be the second to congratulate you, whatever it is . . .

SULLIVAN: *(Opening the note.)* It's from Mr. Gladstone . . .

Piano—"National Anthem"

GLADSTONE: (GROSSMITH) I am permitted by Her Majesty to propose that in recognition of your distinguished talents as a composer . . .

Piano—"March of Peers" A Stage Hand brings on a sword for JESSIE. SULLIVAN *is knighted by* JESSIE. *The Stage Hand exits with the sword.*

CRITIC: (ROSE) Sir Arthur, show yourself the best man in Europe.

CRITIC: (GERALDINE) Sir Arthur, how long is it since you compsed anything worthy of you?

CRITIC: (ROSE) Sir Arthur, your friends have to apologize for you.

CRITIC: (GERALDINE) Sir Arthur, you were knighted to shame you into writing something better than these silly comic operas with that wretched Gilbert.

CRITIC: (GROSSMITH) Some things Dr. Sullivan may do, Sir Arthur Sullivan may not do . . .

CRITIC: (JESSIE) It will look very odd to read that a new comic opera is in preparation by W. S. Gilbert and Sir Arthur Sullivan.

All exit except JOE *and* SULLIVAN. SULLIVAN *goes to sit on the podium.*

JOE: We regret to announce that Sir Arthur Sullivan fainted when he presented himself on the stage of the Savoy last night to receive the congratulations of the audience for *Princess Ida.* The following bulletin has been posted: "Sir Arthur has passed a quiet night, and although in pain he is on the whole better. Absolute rest and quietude has been enjoined by his doctors."

JOE *exits.*

SULLIVAN: Hmmmm.

CARTE *enters and goes to his table.* GERALDINE *(As* HELEN*) enters and gives him a letter.*

HELEN: It's from Sullivan.

CARTE: Oh, good, I hope he's feeling better now.

CARTE *peruses the letter with growing consternation.*

SULLIVAN: I regret to have to inform you that I am not going to write any more music for comic opera . . .

CARTE *looks across at* HELEN.

HELEN: I've been expecting it.

CARTE: Oh, he must be tired, after being so ill. But we'd better go and see him. The *Princess Ida* receipts are dropping already.

HELEN: Yes, but I should go easy with him. It may be more serious than you think it is.

HELEN *and* CARTE *go to* SULLIVAN, *who rises.*

HELEN: It's good to see you looking so much better, Arthur.

CARTE: Yes, worried about you, Arthur. Very worried . . .

SULLIVAN: Well I'm in less pain now. A rest and a trip away will put me right, and then I can start to think about the future . . .

HELEN: A good idea . . .

CARTE: But there is of course, the question . . .

HELEN: *(Quickly.)* Where are you going?

SULLIVAN: I thought I might go to Paris for a while and then on to Brussels . . .

HELEN: It's good to get away and forget everything . . .

SULLIVAN: *(Guiltily.)* I'm sorry about my letter, Richard.

CARTE: Oh, I can understand how you feel, Arthur, you've been under such tremendous pressure. Don't worry, *Princess Ida* will hold up for a few weeks until you are feeling better. Gilbert is already working on a new libretto . . .

SULLIVAN: It won't concern me.

CARTE: *(With a smile.)* I refuse to take you seriously at the moment . . .

SULLIVAN: That is my last word. No more comic opera. *(He sits.)*

CARTE: We'll see. We'll see . . .

HELEN *and* CARTE *move back to the the table.* CARTE's *mood changes right away.*

CARTE: He must write another score. He is under contract

HELEN: And *Princess Ida* will have to come off soon. And we have nothing to take its place.

CARTE: We'd better write to Sullivan. Where is he now?

HELEN: Brussels.

She picks up a pad and pencil, and sits. CARTE *dictates a letter to her.*

CARTE: "Business, as you will have observed, shows signs of

falling off. By our arrangement I have to give you six month's notice in case of a new piece being required. Please accept this note as fulfilling the necessary formality. I have already sent a copy of this note to Gilbert.'

HELEN *exits.* GILBERT *enters, reading a note.*

SULLIVAN: *(Writing to* CARTE) "My dear Carte, it is *impossible* for me to do another piece of those already written by Gilbert and myself . . . "

GILBERT: *(Writing to* SULLIVAN) "Dear Sullivan, I am amazed at your attitude. You are aware by our five-year agreement we are *bound* to supply Carte with a new opera on receiving from him six month's notice, and, if we fail to do so we are liable to him for any losses that may result from our default . . . "

SULLIVAN: *(Writing to* GILBERT) "With *Princess Ida,* I came to the end of my tether with that kind of piece. The music is never allowed to speak for itself."

GILBERT: *(Writing to* SULLIVAN) "Your reflections on the character of the libretto I have supplied you with causes me much pain. I enclose a new libretto.

SULLIVAN: *(Reading.)* " . . . and the hero, a mountebank, swallows a . . . *(he drops the script)* lozenge . . . " Don't you see? I'm tired of all that. We must break new ground. Don't you see? I want something of importance to work on.

GILBERT, *having thought it over, telephones* SULLIVAN, *who lifts his receiver.*

GILBERT: Sullivan, I'm completely at a loss to know what you want from me. The best thing to do is find someone else to write a libretto for you . . .

SULLIVAN: Simply because your libretto does not seem to furnish me suitable musical suggestions, doesn't mean we should grind to a standstill . . .

GILBERT: Find someone else, damn you!

Off-stage voices are heard.

JESSIE: *(Off.)* Sir Arthur Sullivan and Mr. Gilbert look like splitting for the simple reason that they cannot find a story.

GROSSMITH: *(Off.)* The great question of the day is: Are Gilbert and Sullivan played out?

JOE: *(Off.)* Is there any truth in the rumour that Richard D'Oyly Carte is about to launch a competition to find Gilbert and Sullivan a script?

GERALDINE: *(Off.)* What is happening at the Savoy?

JESSIE: *(Off.)* Is D'Oyly Carte's Empire about to collapse?

CARTE: *(Rising and pacing between* GILBERT *at his desk and* SULLIVAN *on the podium.)* Arthur, things are getting desperate. You must have heard what people are saying. We must have a new piece.

SULLIVAN: I am not writing for a lozenge!

CARTE: Is that all that is holding us up?

SULLIVAN: I am not writing for a lozenge!

CARTE: Gilbert has told me he has provided you with a plot and you refuse to work on it.

SULLIVAN: Yes, but it is the same old plot he keeps trying to fob off on me.

CARTE: Surely it will do?

SULLIVAN: Look, Carte, if he will find another subject, I—I will write the music. But I am not writing for a lozenge.

GILBERT: The time has come when I must state with great reluctance that I cannot construct another plot for your next opera.

SULLIVAN: Further discussion is useless. I regret it very much.

CARTE: Gilbert, I'll sue you for every penny I can get out of you.

GILBERT: Damn and blast you, Carte. Don't come threatening me. Sue me? I'll sue you for malicious behavior. It is Sullivan you ought to attack, he turns all my ideas down.

CARTE: *(Punctured.)* I know, I know . . .

GILBERT: Don't keep saying "I know, I know" all the time, it is exceedingly tedius.

CARTE: But, Gilbert, old man, you must have other ideas.

GILBERT: I have not another blasted idea in my head.

CARTE: Look, I hate to remind you of your contract . . .

GILBERT: *(Rising and taking a Japanese sword from his umbrella stand in mistake for his walking-stick.)* Damn, damn you I've given him a plot!

SULLIVAN: I'm not writing for a lozenge!

GILBERT: Now look here, Sullivan . . .

GILBERT, *still waving the sword, comes running towards the podium.* SULLIVAN *rises and runs away.* CARTE *tries to calm them and then exits. Piano—"The Mikado".* GILBERT *looks at the sword: inspiration dawns!*

GILBERT: Sullivan! Sullivan! No, no, come back, don't go away, now . . .

SULLIVAN: *(Shouting.)* Get way, you madman!

GILBERT: *(Continuing to chase* SULLIVAN *round and round the podium.)* Stand still, no more lozenges—it'll have a Japanese setting. Call it *The Mikado*—or *The Town of Titipu.* We'll have a joke at all the japanning that's going on . . .

SULLIVAN *stops, exhausted.*

GILBERT: We'll go to the Japanese village in Knightsbridge and find someone, Japanese, to coach the actors in deportment.

GILBERT *begins to mince around: watched by a frightened and astonished* SULLIVAN.

GILBERT: Miya Suma, miya Suma.

SULLIVAN: Er—quite.

GILBERT *advances on* SULLIVAN, *who—still not convinced that* GILBERT *is all right—backs away a little.*

GILBERT: Costumes colourful, especially made of pure silk—at Liberty's in Regent Street. But the principals' costumes we'll get from Japan, the real thing—ancient . . . Samurai. We'll have armour . . .

SULLIVAN: The Japanese are rather small—on the whole—that's only a point—not a criticism. Armour might not fit . . .

GILBERT: All right, scrap the armour. We don't need armour. But it all appeals to you . . . ?

SULLIVAN: Why not? Why not . . . ?

The Company come on for "The Mikado" Sequence carrying fans.

THE MIKADO

ALL: Behold the Lord High Executioner!
   A personage of noble rank and title—
A dignified and potent officer,
   Whose functions are particularly vital!
      Defer, defer,
   To the Lord High Executioner! Defer, defer,
   To the Noble Lord
   To the Lord High Executioner!

"TIT WILLOW"

KO-KO: (SULLIVAN) On a tree by a river, a little tom tit,
Sang willow, tit-willow, tit-willow.
And I said to him, dickey bird
Why do you sit? Singing willow, tit-willow, tit-willow?
Is it weakness of intellect, birdy, I cried,
Or a rather tough worm in your little inside?
With shake of his poor little head
He replied . . . Oh . . .

"THREE LITTLE MAIDS"

GIRLS: Three little maids from school we are,
Pert as a schoolgirl well can be,.
Filled to the brim with girlish glee,
    Three little maids from school!

YUM-YUM: Everything is a source of fun. *(Chuckle.)*

PEEP-BO: Nobody's safe, for we care for none! *(Chuckle.)*

PITTI-SING: Life is a joke that's just begun! *(Chuckle.)*

ALL: Three little maids from school! *(Dancing.)*
Three little maids who, all unwary,
Come from a ladies' seminary,
Freed from its genius tutelary—*(Suddenly demure.)*
Three little maids from school!

"A WANDERING MINSTREL I"

NANKIPOO: A wandering minstrel I—
A thing of shreds and patches,
of ballads, songs and snatches,
    And dreamy lullaby!

"HERE'S A HOWDEDO!"

YUM-YUM: (JESSIE) Here's a howdedo. If I marry you
When your time has come to perish

Then the maiden whom you cherish
(Must be slaughtered too!)
(Repeat "Here's a howdedo"—twice.)

KO-KO: (GROSSMITH) Here's a pretty mess. In a month or less
I must die without a wedding
Let the bitter tears I'm shedding
Witness my distress.
(Here's a pretty mess) *(Repeat twice.)*
(Here's a state of things!) *(Repeat twice.)*

KO-KO: Here's a state of thing. To her life she clings
Matrimonial devotion doesn't seem to suit her notion
Burial it brings!

"THE MOON AND I"

KATISHA: (ROSE) Ah! Pray make no mistake
We are not shy
We're very wide awake
The moon and I.
(Repeat the last two lines.)

"FOR HE'S GOING TO MARRY YUM-YUM"

CARTE: For he's going to marry Yum-Yum, Yum-Yum,
Your anger pray bury
For all will be merry
I think you had better succumb,
And join our expressions of glee.

GROSSMITH: On this subject I pray you be dumb, dumb, dumb,
You'll find there are many who'd wed for a penny
The word for your guidance is mum, mum, mum
There's lots of good fish in the sea.

CHORUS: On the subject we pray you be dumb, dumb, dumb,
We think you had better succumb, cumb, cumb,
You'll find.

Scream.

"MY OBJECT ALL SUBLIME"

MIKADO: (GILBERT) The advertising quack who wearies
  With tales of countless cures,
    His teeth, I've enacted,
    Shall all be extracted
  By terrified amateurs.
The music-hall singer attends a series
  Of masses and fugues and "ops"
    By Bach, interwoven
    With Spohr and Beethoven,
At classical Monday Pops.

The billiard sharp whom anyone catches,
  His doom's extremely hard—
    He's made to dwell—
    In a dungeon cell
  On a spot that's always barred.
And here he plays extravagent matches
  In fitless finger-stalls
    On a cloth untrue,
    With a twisted cue
And elliptical billiard balls! HA! HA!
  My object all sublime
  I shall achieve in time—
To let the punishment fit the crime—
  The punishment fit the crime;
  And make each prisoner pent
  Unwillingly represent
A source of innocent merriment!
  Of innocent merriment!

"THE FLOWERS THAT BLOOM IN THE SPRING"

GROSSMITH: The flowers that bloom in the spring,
  Tra la,
  Breathe promise of merry sunshine—
As we merrily dance and we sing,
  Tra la,

We welcome the hope that they bring,
  Tra la,
Of a summer of roses and wine.
And that's what we mean when we say that a thing
Is welcome as flowers that bloom in the spring.
  Tra la la la la la, etc.
The flowers that bloom in the spring.

ALL: Tra la la la, etc. *(Refer to score.)*

"DERRY DOWN"

ALL: If that is so, sing derry down derry
It's evident very our tastes are one
Away we'll go and merrily marry
Nor tardily tarry till day is done. *(Repeat.)*

Sing derry down derry,
We'll merrily marry
Nor tardily tarry
'Til day is done.

All exit except CARTE *and* GILBERT, *who go to their places.* JOE *returns with a newspaper which he gives to* CARTE.

JOE: Twentieth October, eighteen eighty-six. With *The Mikado* a success all over the world. Some people enjoy reading their morning papers. Mr. Carte! . . . *(He goes to* GILBERT *and gives him a paper.)* Others do not!

JOE *exits.*

GILBERT: Carte. *(He goes to* CARTE.)

CARTE: Ah, Gilbert. I see *The Mikado* has broken all records in New York.

GILBERT: Where's the music for *Ruddigore*? I've been trying to pin him down for weeks. He's never in. Every time I open a newspaper, what do I find? "Sir Arthur Sullivan attends

Royal Garden Party." "Sir Arthur Sullivan at Ascot." "Sir Arthur Sullivan at Henley." "Sir Arthur Sullivan with Mrs. Ronalds." So much for all the work he is supposed to be doing. *(He returns to his desk.)*

SULLIVAN *enters. Picks up telephone.* GILBERT *hits his desk.*

GILBERT: Where is the music for *Ruddigore?*

SULLIVAN: *(On his telephone.)* Sorry, Bertie, another interruption . . . Yes, of course you shall have the Jubilee Ode by the end of the month. I've been so busy with my oratorio . . . She said what? . . . Oh, how very kind . . . Yes of course, *her* will is my . . . Yes. Good-bye. *(He replaces the receiver. To* CARTE.*)* The Queen has just asked me to write a grand opera, she said I'd do it so well . . .

CARTE *and* GILBERT *rise and go to* SULLIVAN.

GILBERT: Where's the music for *Ruddigore* . . . ?

SULLIVAN: What?

GILBERT: Where is it?

CARTE: *(Apologetically)* Arthur, we hope to go into rehearsals next week. May we see some of it?

SULLIVAN: Umm.

GILBERT: Please?

SULLIVAN: Well, umm.

An awkward silence.

GILBERT: You haven't even started on it, have you?

CARTE: It's too bad, Arthur . . .

GILBERT: Too bad. You had a commitment to us and you spend your time flying your kite. We are supposed to open in a matter of weeks.

SULLIVAN: But I've been very busy . . .

GILBERT: And made yourself ill into the bargain. You look like death warmed up. Damn you, Sullivan. We must cash in on *The Mikado's* success. Tell him, Carte.

CARTE: *(Having weighed up the situation.)* Arthur, I'm very disappointed in you.

GILBERT: Disappointed!

CARTE: We'll have to postpone *Ruddigore*, but please hurry.

GILBERT: For God's sake, Sullivan, hurry.

CARTE *and* GILBERT *exit.*

SULLIVAN: How do you expect me to get through all this work, all of you? Aren't I to be allowed a life of my own? In the space of a year I have to write a comic opera, a hymn tune and an oratorio. What do you think I am? A barrel-organ—you turn the handle and I churn out the music to order? Well, you shall have your comic opera—but I warn you—things are going to change. I will not be dictated to. I will not. I will not . . .

RUDDIGORE

CARTE *enters as* SIR RODERICK.

SIR RODERICK: (CARTE) Beware! Beware! Beware!

ROB: (SULLIVAN) Gaunt vision, who art thou
That thus, with icy glare
And stern relentless brow
Appearest, who knows how?

SIR RODERICK: I am the spectre of the late
Sir Roderick Murgatroyd
Who comes to warn thee that thy fate
Thou canst not now avoid.

ROB: Alas, poor ghost!

SIR RODERICK: The pity you express for nothing goes
We spectres are a jollier crew
Than you perhaps suppose!
Ha! Ha! Ha! Ha!

"THE GHOST'S HIGH NOON"

When the night wind howls in the chimney cowls, and the
    bat in the moonlight flies,
And inky clouds, like funeral shrouds, sail over the
    midnight skies—
When the footpads quail at the night-bird's wail, and
    black dogs bay at the moon,
Then is the spectre's holiday—then is the ghost's high noon!
For then is the ghost's high noon
High noon
Then is the ghost's high noon
As the sob of the breeze sweeps over the trees, and the
    mists lie low on the fen,
From grey tomb-stones are gathered the bones that once
    were women and men,
And away they go, with a mop and a mow, to the revel
    that ends too soon,
For cockcrow limits our holiday—the dead of the night's
    high noon!
The dead of the night's high noon
High noon
The dead of the night's high noon.

ROB: I recognize you now—you are the picture that hangs at
the end of the gallery.

SIR RODERICK: In a bad light I am.

ROB: Are you considered a good likeness?

SIR RODERICK: I am crude in colour, because I have only been
painted for ten years. In two centuries' time I shall be regarded
as an old master and you will be very sorry you spoke so
slightly of me.

ROB: And why, may I ask, have you left your frame?

SIR RODERICK: I have come to remind you that you are evading the conditions under which you are permitted to exist.

The Lights fade. JOE *removes* CARTE'S *"Sir Roderick" cloak. The Lights come up to reveal* SULLIVAN *facing* GILBERT *and* CARTE.

SULLIVAN: What?

CARTE: I said that *Ruddigore* will not run. People have been booing and hissing—crying out "Bring back *The Mikado*". It will not run!

SULLIVAN: Well excuse me, are you blaming me?

GILBERT: Yes. If you'd got down to your work earlier instead of flying your kite, and if you had written music less suited to a cathedral, and more suited to comic opera, the audiences might have enjoyed it more . . .

SULLIVAN: Strange that the music should be under attack—there was so little opportunity for music in *Ruddigore*, people wondered what I had to do with it. It was just a straight play with a few songs thrown in . . .

GILBERT: And half of those should have been cut.

CARTE: Gentlemen, gentlemen, this never gets us anywhere.

GILBERT: If he'd put more effort into it instead of flying his kite . . .

CARTE: Lots of things wrong with it. *Your* title for a start . . . *Ruddigore*—people found it offensive.

GILBERT: What should I have called it? "Kensington Gore?" Or "Not Half So Good As *The Mikado*"? How about that, eh? Or—"Forgive The Music, The Composer Is Only Half With Us"! That's a good one . . .

SULLIVAN: I'm not going to stay here listening to this. I have a boat train to catch. (*He goes to his podium and sits.*)

GILBERT: See what I mean? His work means nothing to him. We are a mere intrusion on his holidays.

CARTE: Go easy on him, Gilbert. He's probably hurt, it's not a happy situation for any of us having a failure on our hands . . .

GILBERT: I don't know what this fuss is about. *Ruddigore*, a failure? It will net me around seven thousand pounds. I could wish for a few more failures like that . . .

CARTE: Yes, but it is still a come down after *The Mikado*. In this business you are only as good as your latest offering. We shall have to think very carefully about the next one.

GILBERT: What does the public want?

JOE enters with a copy of "The Times" for CARTE.

CARTE: Look, we must think upon new lines. *The Mikado* succeeded because it was fresh, it startled people . . . We must think that way again. There was an article in *The Times* the other day. Did you see it? *(To* JOE.*)* Thank you. *(He takes the newspaper. Reading.)* "A real comic opera dealing with neither topsy-turveydom nor fairies would be a great novelty and a more splendid success than anything we are likely to see during the present dramatic season . . . " Why not think on those lines, Gilbert? A good strong plot would keep Sullivan up to the mark, and he does need keeping up to the mark, I agree—and it may also go some way towards satisfying his grand opera—pretensions—just this once . . .

GILBERT: But it wouldn't be comic opera, would it?

CARTE: I'm sure a writer of your talent and experience could write comedy, in such a way that it does not immediately appear like comedy. With some philosophy! Well, after all, there must be some statement *you'd* like to make that would last . . .

GILBERT: Sugar the pill, you mean?

CARTE: Yes.

GILBERT: All right. Just to show that I am not quite the barbaric buffoon I have been called at times, I'll try to do as you have asked. But I rely on you to keep Sullivan up to the mark. *(He sits at his desk.)*

CARTE: You leave Sullivan to me.

CARTE *walks over to* SULLIVAN'S *podium.*

CARTE: Well, Arthur, what do you think of it?

SULLIVAN: I think we've finally won, Richard.

CARTE: I'm glad. I did talk very seriously to him.

SULLIVAN: This new plot of his is very good, very—human. No topsy-turveydom. Historical setting. Tower of London. He got the idea from a poster on the underground railway. I can hardly believe it.

CARTE: Yes, and this may help to pave the way for something of a more serious nature.

SULLIVAN: A real opera—on a big scale?

CARTE: I cannot say more than this at the moment, Arthur, but my new theatre is coming along, it's coming along. It will house only opera—The English Royal Opera Company. I need hardly say, I am expecting a great deal from Sir Arthur Sullivan.

SULLIVAN: Thank you, Richard . . .

CARTE: So do this one with Gilbert, eh? Just to pave the way . . .

SULLIVAN: Yes, all right. *(He goes to the podium.)* Where is he now?

CARTE: Up on Tower Green I should imagine. As you say—I think we've won. *(He goes to his table.)*

The Company enter.

GILBERT: *(Writing.)* When a jester
Is outwitted
Feelings fester

Heart is lead
Food for fishes
Only fitted
Jester wishes
He was dead.

SULLIVAN: *(Suddenly rising.)* Mr. Gilbert! This is a music rehearsal.

GILBERT: *(Rising.)* I am aware of that, sir!

SULLIVAN: You have no right to be here today, sir.

GILBERT: I've as much right as you, sir.

SULLIVAN: Only with *my* permission!

CARTE: *(Rising and moving to them.)* Come on, Gilbert, old man.

GILBERT: You keep out of it and do your sums—money is your game, Carte! Confine your thoughts to money.

CARTE: How dare you!

SULLIVAN: Oh, this is impossible. Give me my coat!

GILBERT: Stay here and *earn* your money.

SULLIVAN: You—you—don't need me! You don't need a musician. What you need is a barrel-organ . . .

GILBERT: Yes—I've already got the monkey!

SULLIVAN: What did you say, sir?

CARTE: I give up! *(He goes to his table.)*

SULLIVAN: *(Pointing across CARTE at GILBERT)* Let me tell you, sir. I am entitled to some respect from *you*!

GILBERT: I'll give you respect when you behave worthily of respect.

The Lights change. GILBERT, SULLIVAN *and* CARTE *freeze.*

JOE: In two day's time Sir Arthur will finally bring himself to speak to Mr. Gilbert.

GILBERT: These shocks and disturbances are far too much for me, let's have no more of them. I'm too old . . .

SULLIVAN: Nonsense . . .

GILBERT: I am, I am a ruin—you should see me—by moonlight. Put a twig of ivy in my hair and an owl under my arm and Tintern Abbey's got nothing on me.

SULLIVAN: Gilbert, I have to confess that there is one song that has beaten me—I'm sorry but I just cannot set it.

GILBERT: If you can't set it, cut it.

SULLIVAN: But the words are so good. We can't lose it.

GILBERT: Which one is it?

SULLIVAN: The one with the "Heighdy" chorus.

GILBERT: Oh, that's a bugger, that one.

SULLIVAN: Look, I know I always ask you to keep your ideas for tunes to yourself, but this time do you think you could give me a clue?

GILBERT: I'll tell you where I got the idea from. It is something I've heard sailors singing down in Cornwall, when I've been on my yacht. I think it is an old carol—it goes something like this.

The piano starts.

THE YEOMEN OF THE GUARD

"THE YEOMAN SONG"

GILBERT: I have a song to sing, O!

ELSIE: (GERALDINE) What is your song, O?

POINT: (SULLIVAN) It is sung to the moon
    By a love-lorn loon,
  Who fled from the mocking throng, O!
It's the song of merryman, moping mum,

Whose soul was sad, and whose glance was glum,
Who sipped no sup, and who craved no crumb,
  As he sighed for the love of a ladye!

ALL: Heighdy! Heighdy!
  Misery me, lackadaydee!
He sipped no sup, and he craved no crumb,
  As he sighed for the love of a ladye!

ELSIE: (GERALDINE) I have a song to sing, O!

POINT: What is your song, O?

ELSIE: It is sung with the ring
  Of the songs maids sing.
Who love with a love life-long, O!
It's the song of a merry maid, nestling near,
Who loved her lord—and who dropped a tear
At the moan of the merryman, moping mum,
Whose soul was sad, and whose glance was glum,
Who sipped no sup, and craved no crumb,
  As he sighed for the love of a ladye

ALL: Heighdy! Heighdy!
  Misery me, lackadaydee!
He sipped no sup, and he craved no crumb,
  As he sighed for the love of a ladye.

All but GILBERT, SULLIVAN *and* CARTE *exit.* SULLIVAN *hands* CARTE *a letter then sits on the podium.*

GILBERT: A what?

CARTE: A cipher.

GILBERT: Give it to me. *(Reading.)* "Except during vocal rehearsals and the two orchestral rehearsals, I am a cipher in the theatre. They are Gilbert's pieces with music added by me. Unless a change is made I should wish to give it up altogether." Of all the confounded . . . *(He paces.).*

CARTE: Calm down, Gilbert. Calm down.

GILBERT: Calm down? Where is Sullivan? Riviera, I suppose. Leaving me to cope with all the real work here. And he says *he*'s the cipher in the theatre. What, pray, am I? The bloody doormat. Doesn't he realize that I have sacrificed my ambition to write these operas? I am a serious dramatist . . .

SULLIVAN: I find comic opera distasteful. It no longer suits me.

GILBERT: All right. All right. Do both.

SULLIVAN: No, I've been a slave to comic opera too long. I do not want to spend any more of my life clothing stock figures in music.

GILBERT: Well, I'm certainly not having my plot, my words drowned in music. Comic opera is bad enough. It's still all Sullivan . . .

SULLIVAN: I have spent the last twelve years of my life sacrificing my music to your words . . .

GILBERT: Sacrifice. Sacrifice. Have I not sacrificed myself for you? Very well, I am sorry if you've been forced to efface yourself in our associations. If you have actually suffered in silence for twelve years, you have nobody to blame but yourself. If we ever meet again, let it not be as master and servant but as master and master . . .

CARTE: (*As* DON ALHAMBRA) As the country is in a state of insurrection, it is absolutely necessary that you assume the reins of government at once: and until it is decided which of you shall be king, I have arranged that you will reign jointly, so that no question shall arise hereafter as to the validity of any of your acts.

SULLIVAN: As one individual?

CARTE: As one individual.

GILBERT: Like this?

CARTE: Yes, that's the way it should be . . .

The Company enter for "The Gondoliers".

THE GONDOLIERS

ANTONIO: (GROSSMITH) For the merriest fellows are we, tra la
(See score for "tralas".)
That ply on the emerld sea, tra la;

CHORUS: With loving and laughing,
   And quipping and quaffing,
We're happy as happy can be, tra la—
   As happy as happy can be!
(Many "tralas", see score for "tralas".)

TESSA: (ROSE) When a merry maiden marries,
Sorrow goes and pleasure tarries;
   Every sound becomes a song,
   All is right, and nothing's wrong!
From today and ever after
Let our tears be tears of laughter
   Every sigh that finds a vent
   Be a sigh of sweet content!

The Company exits after "The Gondoliers", except GILBERT *and* SULLIVAN. *They sit, possibly on a skip.* SULLIVAN *begins to sing "Take a pair of sparkling eyes".* JOE *enters and stands behind* GILBERT *and* SULLIVAN. GILBERT *and* SULLIVAN *sit, looking worn-out, and speak their lines out front.*

"TAKE A PAIR OF SPARKLING EYES"

MARCO: (SULLIVAN) Take a pair of sparkling eyes,
   Hidden, ever and anon,
      In a merciful eclipse—
Do not heed their mild surprise—
   Having passed the Rubicon,
      Take a pair of rosy lips;
Take a figure trimly planned—
   Such as admiration whets
      (Be particular in this);
Take a tender little hand,
   Fringed with dainty fingerettes,

Press it, Press it—in parenthesis;—
Ah! Take all these, you lucky man—
Take and keep them, if you can! *(Etc.)*.

JOE: And after a very successful opening of *The Gondoliers* Mr.
Gilbert will write to Sir Arthur Sullivan . . .

GILBERT: "I must thank you again for the magnificent work
you have put into the piece. It gives one a chance of shining
right through into the twentieth century with reflected light."

JOE: And Sir Arthur Sullivan will reply to Mr. Gilbert.

SULLIVAN: "Don't talk of reflected light. In such a perfect book
as *The Gondoliers* you shine with an individual brilliancy which
no other writer can hope to attain. If any thanks are due
anywhere, they should be from me to you."

GILBERT: Take a pretty little cot—
    Quite a minature affair—
        Hung about with trellised vine,
Furnished it upon the spot
    With the treasure rich and rare
        I've endeavoured to define.
Live to love and love to live—
    You will ripen at your ease,
        Growing on the sunny side—
Fate has nothing more to give.
    You're a dainty man to please
        If you are not satisfied.
Ah! Take my counsel, happy man;
Act upon it, if you can!

CARTE *enters with a ledger. He hands it to* JOE, *who takes it to*
GILBERT, *open.*

GILBERT: Carpets?

THE CARPET QUARREL

CARTE: Don't rise your voice to me, Gilbert.

GILBERT: Five hundred pounds for bloody carpets?

CARTE: And don't swear.

GILBERT: Just explain these accounts.

CARTE: They are preliminary expenses for *The Gondoliers.*

GILBERT: I don't see where carpets come into it.

CARTE: Just look what you spent on set and costumes. And I never complained. You never consulted me.

GILBERT: That's beside the point. I don't expect to be stung for bills which have nothing to do with me. Like five hundred pounds for front of house carpets.

CARTE: If you look carefuly, you'll see it's not five hundred but one hundred and forty.

GILBERT: Damn you, Carte, I'm not paying a penny for carpets. They have nothing to do with me . . .

CARTE: You rent this theatre. Our contract states that you share costs in maintaining repairs . . .

GILBERT: The public comes to see my plays, not to gawp at carpets illuminated by electric lamps.

CARTE: I've done everything I can for you. I've lied and told tales, raised money in the early days, everything. I found the best theatre I could—I did the best I could for it. I should just have put sawdust and spitoons down—and left you to it . . .

GILBERT: I demand a new agreement.

CARTE: All right. I'LL raise your rent from four thousand to five thousand pounds.

GILBERT: Then you can find yourself another author.

CARTE: Very well, that is understood. You will write no more for the Savoy.

GILBERT: I made you, Carte. You build an empire, and you

kick away the ladder by which you climbed.

CARTE: *(Sitting at his table.)* Get out of my office.

GILBERT *goes to* SULLIVAN.

GILBERT: Five hundred pounds for carpets. We'll fight him together.

SULLIVAN: Please, Gilbert, I am ill—I don't want to fight anybody. I want to be left alone to work in peace.

GILBERT: You cannot be left in peace while Carte builds his empire at our expense.

SULLIVAN: I don't see the point of destroying everything we've done for a carpet worth a hundred and forty pounds.

GILBERT: *(To* CARTE*)* I shall take you to court, sir.

CARTE: Do so.

SULLIVAN: *(Rising.)* Please, please, I beg you, no more of this. The whole wretched business is making me ill. I can't work. We are making laughing stocks of ourselves. And the Company is going to pieces.

GILBERT: There is a principle at stake here, Sullivan. This man is nothing but a bloody capitalist.

CARTE: *(Rising.)* It amazes me, Gilbert, that you can throw that word at me with impunity. You are a born capitalist. How much money have you made in the last few years?

GILBERT: I've earned it.

CARTE: And you've used others to earn it for you which makes you a capitalist like me. It's always amused me, Gilbert, how in your plays, you've come out against the money-makers, you've supported the poor and down-trodden—and yet you've used everybody for you own ends. And you wouldn't even pay a member of your own company anything like what he is worth. This house of yours at Grim's Dyke. How many servants will it employ there? Forty or more, I'm told.

GILBERT: How many servants do you have? How much money have you made?

CARTE: You, sir, we are talking about you.

GILBERT: I want to talk about you.

SULLIVAN: Stop it, both of you.

GILBERT: You, sir, are an exploiter. You have exploited me, and you have exploited him.

CARTE: Have I exploited you, Arthur?

SULLIVAN: No.

GILBERT: I see. Yes, I see. Carte, I give you notice that you will not perform any libretti of mine after Christmas eighteen ninety. In fact, after the withdrawal of *The Gondoliers* the combined work of Gilbert and Sullivan will be heard no more.

CARTE: So be it.

The Company enter. JOE *first.*

FINALE

The remaining actors and actresses speak out the following: taking each line in turn.

JOE: And all for one hundred and forty pounds!

The piano starts.

JESSIE: Gilbert will take Carte to court—and put in an Official Receiver to check the account.

GROSSMITH: There will be two more Savoy operas. Both will fail.

JOE: Both will write with other collaborators—both will have less success.

JESSIE: Gilbert will eventually stage his "Lozenge Play"—it will have two hundred and twenty-nine performances.

ROSE: Sullivan will realize his dream—his opera *Ivahoe*—at Carte's new Opera House . . .

GERALDINE: But it will play only one hundred and forty performances.

ROSE: Queen Victoria, after suggesting that Sullivan should write an opera, will not actually go to see it.

GERALDINE: But she will call for a private performance of *The Gondoliers* at Windsor Castle.

JOE: And the Royal Opera House, Carte's great ambition—will become the Palace Theatre—the home of—musical comedy.

JESSIE: Gilbert's gout will get worse.

GERALDINE: Sullivan's kidney disease will make him weaker.

JOE: After the Twenty-first Birthday performance of *The Sorcerer* they will enter from different sides of the stage, bow to the audience, speak not a word to each other: leave the theatre separately and never see each other again.

ROSE: Twenty-second November nineteen hundred: finally beaten by the kidney disease that has wrecked his life, Sullivan will die.

SULLIVAN *exits.*

GERALDINE: Mrs. Ronalds will be just too late to be with him in his final moment.

ROSE: On Queen Victoria's Order he will be buried in St. Paul's.

JESSIE: As the procession passes along the Embankment, D'Oyly Carte will drag himself from his sick bed to the window to see the last of his old friend. And he will have to be carried back to bed.

JOE: Where four months later, he will die.

CARTE *exits.*

JESSIE: Gilbert will live on into the twentieth century.

GROSSMITH: He will become notorious as a Justice of the Peace.

JESSIE: And an even more notorious motorist.

GROSSMITH: And in nineteen hundred and seven, twenty-four years after Sullivan, he will be knighted.

JESSIE: Twenty-ninth May nineteen hundred and eleven, he will go to the rescue of two girls who are swimming in his lake. And he will drown.

GILBERT *exits.*

GERALDINE: He always said he wished to die on a summer's day in his own garden.

JESSIE: He will leave over a hundred thousand pounds.

JESSIE *exits.*

ROSE: Sullivan will leave less than fifty thousand pounds.

ROSE *and* GERALDINE *exit.*

JOE: D'Oyly Carte will leave more than two hundred thousand pounds.

GROSSMITH: But throughout the twentieth century their fame will rest on the operas which will sweep the world—playing in every opera house in every town—and their songs will be the best-known songs.

GROSSMITH *exits.* JOE *sweeps the stage and whistles music as he does so. The Lights slowly fade.*

GILBERT: *(Off.)* I must thank you again for the magnificent work you have put into the piece. It gives one a chance of shining right through into the twentieth century with reflected light.

SULLIVAN: *(Off.)* Don't talk of reflected light. In such a perfect book as *The Gondoliers* you shine with an individual brilliancy which no other writer can hope to attain. If any thanks are due anywhere, they should be from me to you.

CURTAIN

FURNITURE AND PROPERTY LIST

ACT ONE

On stage:

GILBERT:

High desk. *On it:* writing materials, scripts
High backed stool
Umbrella stand with walking stick
Hat stand
Screen

SULLIVAN:

Podium
Music stand, music and baton
Padded seat
Table. *On it:* sheets of music, scores, scripts
Hat stand
Screen

CARTE:

Table. *On it:* writing materials, documents, contracts, scripts
Upright armchair
2 small chairs
Hat stand

Piano, stool and music (on stage or in auditorium)

Off stage:

Broom (JOE)
Music sheet (GROSSMITH)
Music sheets and scores (THE COMPANY)
Courtroom unit for *Trial by Jury*, with books and papers on
Bench   (set by STAGE HANDS)
Tray of filled champagne glasses (JOE)
Card table with "Bombay" pictures, including black one (JOE)
Placards (STAGE HANDS)

Personal:

JOE: Watch

ACT TWO

Set:

Telephone on GILBERT'S table
Telephone on CARTE'S table
Telephone on SULLIVAN'S table
Pad and pencil on CARTE'S table
New libretto on GILBERT'S table
Japanese sword in GILBERT'S umbrella stand

Off stage:

Light bulb on cushion, hammer (JOE)
Opened letter (SULLIVAN)
Tray of filled champagne glasses (JOE)
Note on salver (JOE)
Sword (STAGE HAND)
Letter (GERALDINE)
Fans (THE COMPANY, for *Mikado* sequence)
Newspaper (JOE)
4 newspapers (JESSIE, ROSE, GERALDINE, GROSSMITH)
Copy of *The Times* (JOE)
Letter (SULLIVAN)
Ledger (CARTE)

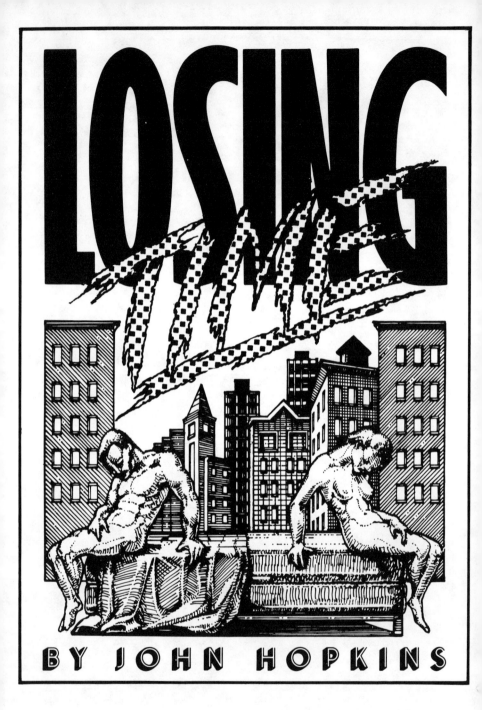

LOSING TIME

BY JOHN HOPKINS

Jane Alexander, Shirley Knight and Tony Roberts won critical acclaim at the award-winning Manhattan Theatre Club for their work in this powerful drama about relationships traumatized by a violent sexual assault. NOTE: Play Contains Explicit Language.

ESCOFFIER
KING OF CHEFS
by
Owen S. Rackleff

In this one-man show set in a Monte Carlo villa at the end of
the last century, the grand master of the kitchen, Escoffier,
ponders a glorious return from retirement. In doing so, he
relates ancedotes about the famous and shares his mouth-wat-
ering recipes with the audience.

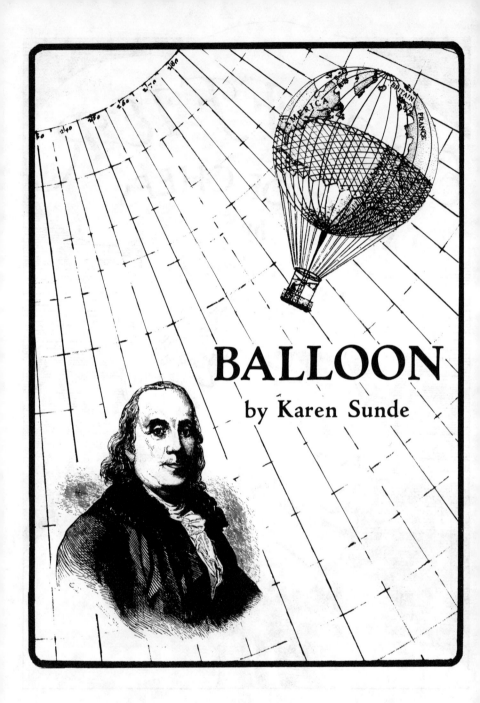

BALLOON

by Karen Sunde

Benjamin Franklin, American Ambassador to Paris during
the 18th Century, plays host to his French contemporaries
during a festive parlor visit, while the fates of nations hang
in the balance.

SOME RAIN

by James Edward Luczak

Set in rural Alabama in 1968, the play is the bittersweet tale of a middle-aged waitress whose ability to love and be loved is re-kindled by her chance encounter with a young drifter. First presented in 1982 at the Eugene O'Neill Playwright's Conference and Off-Broadway on Theatre Row.

LOOKING-GLASS

by Michael Sutton and Cynthia Mandelberg

This provocative chronicle, interspersed with fantasy sequences from ALICE IN WONDERLAND, traces the career of Charles Dodgson (better known as Lewis Carroll) from his first work on the immortal classic, to his downfall when accused of immortality.

DEATH *in the* **POT**

by Manuel Van Loggem

An English-style thriller with a fascinating plot that takes intricate twists and turns, as a husband and wife try to kill each other off, aided by a mysterious Merchant of Death. Mr. Van Loggem's works have been widely produced throughout Europe.

BATTERY

BY DANIEL THERRIAULT

Electricity is the central metaphor and an expressive image
for this unusual love story set in an electrical workshop.